FAITH

LEARNING TO LIVE
Without Fear

WILLIAM H.
CURTIS

International Standard Book Number: 978-1-4507-1880-6

Library of Congress Catalogue Card Number: Available Upon Request

Printed in the United States of America

First Edition, May 2010

Trademarks

All terms mentioned in this book that are known to be or are suspected of
being trademarks or service marks have been appropriately capitalized. Use
of a term in this book should not be regarded as affecting the validity of any
trademark or service mark.

All Biblical text taken from the New International Version (NIV).

Dedication

This book is dedicated to my family for trusting your lives
to the Lord and for being a constant stream of inspiration!
To Mount Ararat for being a church of absolute excellence!
To all those too numerous to mention who have inspired,
challenged and stretched me to believe God for more in ministry.

TABLE OF CONTENTS

Section 1 – Introduction to Faith

Section 2 – Defining Faith

Section 3 – Applying Faith to Daily Life

Section 4 – The Challenges of Faith

Section 1

Introduction to Faith

Chapter One: *Access Granted*

At some point in all of our lives, we do seek God. We seek God as we sit and wait while our children are born, praying that they have ten fingers and ten toes. We seek God when, at a family's darkest hour, we're praying for the recovery of a beloved relative, lying sick in a hospital bed. We even seek God when we take an airplane on a vacation or a business trip, hoping, often with clenched teeth and shallow breath, that the flight is a safe one for us and for those around us. We know what CAN happen in life – the good, the bad – the joyful, the sad. We know what we want to happen – what we need to happen. We just don't always know how to seek God, when to seek God, and how to trust that our faith will bring us to God and, often, to what we need.

What is Faith?

Faith is illogical to the scientific mind.

Faith is the substance of which miracles are made.

Faith is the evidence that God will do all that He has purposed.

Faith is the invisible, substantive barrier that will separate you from the rest.

The writer of Hebrews says that faith is simply:
the substance of things hoped for, the evidence of things not seen
Hebrews 11:1

Faith has substance. It's believing you can make it even in the most harrowing of circumstances because of your reliance on Him. It becomes the building material that your manifested dreams and purpose are made of. Faith is the evidence of what God will do in your life. Faith is active, it moves forward and it becomes the proof of all that God is doing in you. God in His sovereignty has determined that faith would be a crucial element in your relationship with Him. He wants you to walk in faith each and every day, believing that He has the ability to do even more than you'd ever hoped for!

The staple and foundation of spirituality is faith.

The Bible says that, without faith, it is impossible to please God. In fact, any person who would come to God is taught that he or she must first believe that God rewards the one who through faith seeks God with diligence. Many times, in life, those who seek God do so unintentionally – in need – in a moment's desire – and may not even give faith a moment's thought. It is strange to consider that God would make the foundation of our relationship with Him an issue of faith. After all, He knew it would be hard for us to live by faith when faith often stands in conflict with everything our senses and our logical minds tell us is real or reasonable – what we can or should expect.

It is easy to talk faith; it is difficult to actually live faith.

Jesus lived faith, didn't He? We read and study that this abstract of "faith" is worth our attention, our effort, and our fight. After all, Jesus authored our faith and He is the completion of it in many ways. His trust for His Father, that, ultimately, brought about His own death and resurrection is really the inspiration we need to put our trust in the reality of faith, isn't it? What a sacrifice, but what a reward. It is hard, however, to believe that we, humble people and loyal, simple followers, can mimic the actions of one so honorable, so obedient and so perfect as Jesus.

Why faith?

Why doesn't effort, or the pursuit of perfection, or connection, or status, or position or just sheer dogged determination and tenacity get us the same results? Why faith? Faith, some would say, is the only discipline that reveals the authenticity of our relationship with God. It is the only discipline that proves whether you really trust God or not with your life.

This is the argument the devil used when debating with God about Job's loyalty[1]. This argument is clear: the devil tells God – of course he trusts You and serves You and loves You and honors You. Anybody would with these blessings You give him and the protection You place around him, with the prosperity You let flow into his life. No wonder he honors You. With all those realities, those graces, removed, however, will his love for You become conditional? The devil proposes: What if You remove all your protection and he suffers, will he still love You? Further, will he still believe in You? And, isn't this what is proposed to each of us daily? Do we have faith? Do we believe and trust in God?

What the devil did not know was that Job, while living blessed, was also full of faith. And when everything was stripped from him, he still would not abandon his faith and waited for God to make sense out of what he was enduring. He held to his faith and it ensured that, when God lifted the season of his attack and suffering, Job discovered that his latter days with family and blessings were greater than his former days of wealth and happiness. As a direct result of his unfaltering faith, God doubled his blessings, doubled his provisions, doubled his protection, and doubled his prosperity. His faith proved that he wanted God more than anything or anybody else and trusted God – his faith in God – more than he trusted his physical possessions and former prosperity.

Access to God's Grace

Not only is your faith critical because it speaks to your relationship with God, but faith is critical because it is faith that Paul says gives you access to God's grace. We see this in Paul's letter to the church in Rome, defending the issue of being justified by faith[2]. In other words, you do not earn the right to a relationship with God and, further, your inherent sinning nature would always prevent you from having that relationship with God; therefore, God justified loving all humans and blessing them all by sending Jesus to die for the sins of humanity and to declare all righteous on the basis of Jesus' obedience to His father. It is up to us – to you – to maintain this relationship and to stay faithful. Jesus died for the sins of all man and never once thought about letting Humanity live so as to incur God's wrath. It is important to remember that God loves, blesses and protects you because of Jesus. He awaits you in heaven because of Jesus. He even speaks to you because of Jesus, and He will grant you eternity because of Jesus. It is these sometimes mystical, elusive ideas that make our faith waver at times. Does God speak to us? Is God waiting for us? Again, how do we obtain that access to faith? How do we, unconditionally, become one of the truly faithful? With all of this said and documented, there is nothing in your life that is more critical to who you are and to where you are headed and to how you are to get there than having a relationship with Jesus Christ. He is the reason God will grant you access into His will. It is through His actions and by His death and resurrection that you get your opportunity to commit to faith.

In Romans 5:2, Paul says that precisely what faith gives us is access – access to God and all His graces. He says, through Christ and by faith, we have gained this grace, in which we find ourselves as Christians. Grace is truly God's favor unmerited. The favor that credits righteousness to us through our trust in God is the grace Paul is talking about. Consider Abraham[4] who was not considered by God as righteous because of his adherence to the law for most of his life. In his old age, when he and Sarah had a son, however, his belief and trust in God were finally aptly demonstrated, and God rewarded him.

Forbearance and Sins

This is an interesting dichotomy and does present a bit of a logical problem. Paul is talking about Jesus as the pathway to your faith – the very thing that grants you access to faith and what leads you to God and the favor of righteousness. Abraham is the Bible's champion of faith. However, how, then, is Abraham considered righteous when he dies before Jesus is born, crucified for our sins and resurrected? How can Jesus' death declare Abraham righteous? How, then, is Abraham affected or given access to faith by Jesus' death? His experience with God predates Jesus. According to Paul, righteousness is Abraham's because what God exercises is His **forbearance** – His patience or restraint; in other words, He holds judgment on Abraham's sins until after Jesus is crucified and resurrected and then charges Abraham's sins to Jesus. This is one of His many gifts to humanity, and through faith, it is yours.

In Romans 4:21-25, Paul makes it clear that righteousness only comes through faith in Christ. In Verse 25, God presents Jesus as a sacrifice of atonement through faith in His own blood for us – for humanity. And why? Is it because He is just and sin does not go unpunished or without penance of some kind? Is it because He loves us and allows forbearance, trusting that we will give Him, our God, the gift of faith? Yes. In His forbearance, He leaves the sins committed by those before Jesus unpunished, trusting us with our ability to have faith, by punishing Jesus, for us, so that we might be considered righteous. What a gift. And all we need is faith in Jesus to accept this remarkable gift.

What does "access " to this faith really mean?

Is it simply a way of entry? As Christians, we need to consider it the privilege of entrance – entrance to God's grace. It is our admission ticket into the kindness of God. That is tremendous, the fact that simply your belief and trust in God – not your worship, not your hard work, not your prayer – your simple belief in Him connects you to His infinite kindness. God wants you so near Him, and He knows you can't get there on your own, so He makes a way – He makes it easy for you. It should be easy to love, believe and have faith in Him.

Recently, as I was traveling, I had a small epiphany. I thought about how daily, as we eat our breakfast, buy our favorite latte in the corner coffee shop, or visit the neighborhood grocery store, we see examples of others "making ways", creating pathways or easy access to certain situations for us and for others. As I stood in the airport, in a line full of people – people with the same right of admission that I had – I noticed the ticket checker, a man with whom I have a friendly relationship. When he saw me, he gestured to me, moved me past several people to get my paperwork checked and sent me on the way to my flight. I thought then how he had created a way to bring me near to him, to my destination, to my goal. My simple friendly relationship with him created a convenient access to where I needed to go and what I needed to do. My past friendship with him and the trust and faith I had always had in him as a person led to a situation in which he was holding the power and he extended to me a kindness that spoke volumes – and… allowed me access to my destination. My ticket didn't deserve it – it was like everybody else's – but my proven relationship and my trust in this man made me special that day. We can all be special to God everyday.

Your faith creates access into the kingdom of God.

We have access through faith into this grace, this kindness, this kingdom of God – and… this is truly powerful. It is God's forbearance – His patience – the judgment He withholds for your sins until He can get you to trust in Jesus that allows for this tremendous opportunity. When you trust in Jesus, God freely moves your offenses to Jesus and you don't pay the penalty yourself. In committing to this simple gesture – adapting this easy and faithful belief system as your own, kindness becomes pure delight and pleasure for Christians – believers – in God's love. You will live righteous and die free of sin simply by believing in God's graces and by accepting Jesus as your savior, who died so that you can live free.

Have you ever wondered why God didn't really "get you" for something you did that wasn't unkind, impure or un-Christian? Maybe you sinned in a way that you never had before and sat, waiting for His wrath, scared, sure that He would, in fact, "get you". And it never comes – this wrath; in fact, He appears to " let you off the hook". Did He miss this little slip of yours? No. He didn't miss it. He just exercised the **forbearance** that we've explored here. He knew you would develop faith in Jesus, enough that He could give admission into righteousness based upon your attachment to Jesus and that would produce a better you, a better Christian, a better human being. He trusts you this much. It is your turn to trust Him. Again, it is that simple.

If you ever need a reason to worship God, do so because God wants to be kind to you and is waiting on you to give Him a reason to give you this access to His good graces. If it were anybody else at any given time asking for simple kindness in order to grant you what you want and need – the guy on the corner selling hot dogs wants a simple "hello, how are you?" and you get a free lunch – the little kids selling lemonade on the curb want just a penny and you get a cool, refreshing drink – You would do it, wouldn't you? Pay that penny – ask the man how he's doing. Can you give God your faith in Jesus? Can you accept His kindness and His good graces? Yes, you can. He is looking for the faith you have in Jesus – nothing more, nothing less. He just needs to see that you trust Jesus for your life, and He will trust you with what He has in store for your life.

Real-life applications.

So do you get it? You access grace, you access kindness, and you get admission into the presence of God. He wants so badly to be good to you that He creates an "out" for Himself; He says – accept Jesus and I won't destroy you. Now, this concept is actually heavily doctrinal and I'm sure you're asking, how can I apply this to my own life? After all, we read the Bible verses – we know what is expected of us – we just don't know how to apply it daily – to ourselves – to others through our actions.

Isn't the greater question, however, really – how can I become converted to the idea? The most important spiritual conversion for Christians to go through is to be converted to living a life of faith. We all think, on occasion, will my trust in God give me access to greater things? As we explore that concept here, the answer is – absolutely! Yes! Your happiness, the pathway from your troubles, the ascension out of your despair, the only way things will start looking up again, better again, brighter again – is by having faith in God.

Is this idea new? No, it's been there all along. We just don't give it a lot of thought in our daily lives. Paul has been telling us this all along[5]. Listening to others rather than talking to God, feeling sorry for yourself rather than declaring "enough is enough!" like you didn't have access to this grace – this kindness, this righteous life born of faith in and love for God and Jesus Christ. The moment you decide to start believing God and trusting in Him, you can start eliminating chaos and start receiving kindness.

Spiritual defiance and your path to a better life.

Faith is actually spiritual defiance. It is righteous rebellion against your own "messed up" reality. In Abraham's case[6], it was defying time and age to believe that God wanted to be kind to him by giving him a son in his old age. It didn't make sense at the time, but faith and patience made it so.

What is it in your life that has you penned to the mat of discouragement and has you detached from joy? When are you going to decide to fight back and get up off your back – off that defeatist mat – with the declaration that " if my life is this messed up, I must not be living in the inheritance of my faith, because I'm not looking anymore for a life that's kind". And – why not? Hopefully, that is what you will begin asking yourself.

You have privilege of approach. Why are you still carrying this burden that your life is not what you want it to be? Why are you still dealing with this chaos and lack of joy? Your faith in Christ gives Him the freedom to walk you into God's presence.

Kids do this unconditionally. Maybe we should get back to our roots and make this access possible. For example, my grade school-age daughter had a friend over to the house one day. That Saturday, I was reading over my sermon, which happens to be a Saturday morning routine. I heard the two girls negotiating what they were going to do, and they decided that they were going to turn on some music and dance. I heard my daughter say, "Let's go ask my Dad to dance". Her friend said, hesitantly, "You go ask him. I can't ask the Pastor to dance!" My daughter said, "Come with me. Of course we can ask him to dance, because here, he's just Daddy, and we can ask him to dance."

That's what Jesus does for us. We see ourselves as failures; why would God want to talk to me, bless me, rest His presence with me? Jesus says – trust in Me then, ... get God to dance with you. You have faith in Me. I have relationship with Him. He'll dance with you.

Endnotes

1 Job 1:6-8

2 Romans 3:28

3 Romans 5:2

4 Hebrews 11:8

5 Romans 5

6 Romans 4

Chapter 2: *Living By Faith*

We all try to live a good life. We make mistakes, but, for the most part, we tow the line – work hard, play when we can, pay our bills, feed our families. We want our loved ones to be safe and happy, and we want to live well. Above all, we want to be good people. It is hard, then, to accept illness, financial strife, marital issues and more – all when we've worked to live a righteous and good life. We give money to food banks, we love our families, and we go to church – why, then, does it seem that life isn't always "fair" – that God has often abandoned us in our time of need? It is faith, however, that will see us through these hard times, and that, in and of itself, is often a hard thing to accept.

The staple of our religion and the foundation of our spirituality is faith.

The Bible says we are saved by grace but its through faith that this occurs, which is, for us, a gift given to us by God. We need faith both to trust God and to please Him. It is what many have called, the Christian's sixth sense – and rightly so.

What all of us need to strengthen our lives, to understand the purpose of our lives, to function and flow in our gifts, to handle our obstacles, to fight our enemies, and to defeat our weaknesses is faith. For all of these issues, the foundation regarding how we address each is an issue of faith.

If we entirely understood faith, we would know what we possess to address every area of our lives. If we could activate faith, we could watch areas of our lives begin to transform. If we relied on faith, we would not reach for, grasp or depend on what takes us from God but rather, we would look to God for guidance. If we fully lived by faith, we could truly overcome weaknesses, triumph over temptation, learn to look at ourselves differently and live victoriously. What separates most of us from fulfilling the will of God is faith. What prevents most of us from completing the work of God is faith. What blocks most of us from receiving all the promises of God is faith.

If we fully lived by faith, we could truly overcome weaknesses, triumph over temptation, learn to look at ourselves differently and live victoriously.

Re-introducing yourself to faith.

I want to work backwards to re-introduce you to faith simply because most Christians learn faith's characteristics by studying passages like Hebrews 11 and looking at heroes of faith. We are taught through these "heroes" that faith looks like this:

- It is a sacrifice as our presentation or offering to God.
- It is righteousness as a standard of living for the Christian.
- It is radical obedience.
- It is volunteering to be the only one doing what you are doing because it is for God.

In Hebrews, we are given a look at faith in chapter 11. Chapter 11 gives us a history lesson on how faith looks and how it lives. Chapter 12 opens by saying these witnesses of faith surround us, let's run the race set before us. It does not mean that these heroes of faith are watching us run; the suggestion simply exists that we have enough examples of how faith lives, how faith functions, how faith responds and how faith reacts. So, when we face the challenges that occur daily in our lives, we can draw on these examples to be motivated and not to forsake faith.

If we are honest, faith will come. However, for many of us, this is not enough. It is incomplete; it is shaky. How do we know what faith looks like when we are facing a life that shakes our faith – makes us feel like honesty and other virtuous intentions are not enough. Something must be done, right? I am honest. I do work hard. Why, then, am I making house repairs – why, then, do those around me still get sick – why, then, do I feel empty or afraid? These simple suggestions of honesty or faith are often not enough to keep us motivated with so much, apparently, against us. It is not enough to keep us encouraged, is it? Life can hit you hard and, without encouragement, how do you move on? Do you sometimes find yourself in a place where what is hitting you is so draining and devastating that you respond almost like you have never met God in your life? Have you ever faced something so difficult that it made you wish you could either end life or start life over again?

One may ask why it appears in culture that we are seeing less faith rather than more faith. We have wrestled with the challenges of faith – we have tried to live it, but we have done so without really understanding faith's origin. Where did it come from and why is it here? Why is it that we need faith to please God? Why not effort, why not willingness, why is faith what pleases God? You can't understand the operation of faith nor the potential it can grant for your life without first understanding where it comes from and why it exists. As is stated in Hebrews 11, we are to fight life with faith by knowing we are not the first ones to handle this fight; other people of faith have fought the same battle. And, this is encouraging.

Fear, frustration, failure, fractures, weaknesses, temptations, doubts, lust, greed, envy, jealousy, bitterness, malice, arrogance and more all work against us in our journey to true faith. Hebrews 11 tells us that others have fought these evils and were commended by God for a battle well fought. Like us, they were commended even though they weren't perfect. They were, however, clearly commended for their faith. It is not time to stop running because you face these obstacles; others have had to and still many will have to in the future.

Of course, these temptations and distractions and annoyances are powerful and, often, move us from our righteous and faithful path; that doesn't mean we "accept defeat". Allow these realities to get your attention then move to conquer them with your sheer will and faith. Others have walked before you and done the same. You are not alone; you should be encouraged by those who have triumphed and survived before you. Usually, this is where we stop – in that place where doubt and fear creep in, and these obstacles seem insurmountable. And these challenges take many forms – from a devastating reality like the death of a loved one or the loss of worldly possessions to the simple ups and downs of everyday life like the kids not behaving or a work relationship that has gone horribly wrong. This is why faith is not more prevalent these days but is less prevalent – because, for some reason, we don't think we have the fortitude to go on when we actually do possess such strength. This needs to stop. In Hebrews 12:2 it is written that, after you remember this, and get motivated, knowing that there are those who have run before you, FIX your eyes on Jesus, the "author" and "finisher" of your faith and you will make it! We need to live by this more often.

Back to the origin of faith.

Where does faith come from? How did it get here? Why this abstract concept, as opposed to something else more concrete that you feel or see more profoundly and use in order to know God, live for him and respond to this world? How do you strengthen faith when it's weak, increase faith when you need more of it, and why should you fight so hard for faith? It is, after all, hard to hold and to protect such an abstract and elusive concept.

FIX your eyes on Jesus, the "author" and "finisher"

of your faith and you will make it!

Jesus is the "author" of our faith. The Bible says He is the author of faith – from ancient times – before we translated all that we know of scripture into English – He was always the "author" of faith. Here's what we need to understand about that:

- We have always been asked to fix our eyes on Jesus – to look away from all else – and focus only on Jesus.
- We need to know that author means, "founder" of "our faith" or "leader of our faith". Jesus is the founder and leader of this faith.
- We need to remember that "finisher" means the "completer of our faith".

If, before we address everything in our lives – the good, the bad – the trying days – the days that are wonderful – we trust in faith, and we remember Jesus is behind us – and we understand all those who have gone before us – we can conquer the bad and embrace the good. So – before you respond to any issue, any challenge – look away from it and look at Jesus and let your vision become fixed on Jesus. This is where we will find our guidance and our true path.

I think we'll all admit that whenever we have not responded to something in faith, it is because we look at Jesus AND at what is challenging us spiritually and we let what we are facing compete with our vision of Jesus until it intimidates us and makes us take the wrong steps – the wrong path. Faith is not, first, acting a certain way, or feeling a certain way but it is looking a certain way – directing your quest for answers the right way before proceeding. Pause, think, reflect and move in the appropriate way. Jesus and the many "heroes" of faith from the past are with you.

Why did our "founder" of faith choose this abstract and difficult path as His way to live with God and for God in this world? After all, He had other options – just as we do! Why didn't He choose religious repetition, or active recitation – something more visibly in honor or homage to our God? Why simple, attainable faith? Faith is an active and personal movement to God. Because it is an individual effort, it exudes confidence, trust, and reliance. Faith comes from the Greek work **"PISTIOS"**, which means to win over or to persuade[1]. It is a powerful, personal thing. It is God winning over your confidence by showing you Jesus until what is attacking your faith is defeated. You activate your faith by fixing your eyes on Him and by choosing not to look at anything else but Jesus.

Do you feel faced with something difficult or challenging right now? Is it hard to decide the right response? Do you want to respond to it in faith? Right now, consciously choose not to look at what you are fighting but, instead, fix your eyes on Jesus and while you are seeing Him, He will win over what is challenging your thinking, emotions and behavior and, thereby, you will win – you will transform.

A number of years ago, when Hurricane Katrina swept in and devastated the beautiful, diverse, historic and well-populated city of New Orleans, Louisiana, taking with it the lives, memories, jobs and homes of the good people there, the survivors were able to live past the storm and the aftermath. Keep in mind; they weren't always comforted by the responses of those around them. How could they be comforted and made to believe they would rise again when there was so much working against the recovery efforts – so many comments and flippant remarks that needed to be ignored? While many people poured their hearts and souls into the rescue effort and sent food, medical supplies, money and more, there were still some shockingly terrible people whose behavior terrified many. Where do you look in these times of devastation and confusion? You look to Jesus, and you see and feel the love of someone who stills the storm and whatever is challenging your faith. Jesus is your constant – where you look for how to respond to anything. Use this knowledge to please God and to make it through life.

A foundation.

The foundation to living for God and living the way He wants you to live is having trust in God and confidence in God and, without those qualities, you will fail most tests in life. The "founder" of this faith – this trust, as we discussed, knows that you can handle everything that comes your way, and you can respond to everything that challenges, enrages or confuses you if you train yourself to live trusting God. I know some of you have convinced yourself that you have found a better way, but your "founder" chose faith, and this choice was made with knowledge of the other options. He knew other techniques could get you close, get you in the neighborhood, but He chose faith because only faith could get you through it all and then get you into heaven. Logical thought, reasoning it all out until you can't think anymore, riding it out or even running away, as we discussed previously, will not do the same; these techniques will get you through the moment, the day – but not a lifetime – and… certainly not into heaven. Remember, the "author" and the "founder" of your faith has secured your destiny. Choose His path; make His foundation yours.

Author means, in this case, "prince leader" or, translated, "captain of salvation"[2]. In this way, your "author", Jesus, fought first, and His very existence and His tried and true victory are absolute signs that His method works: Faith is believing by conviction that Jesus' way is the best way and that it works. He was not just an analyst who now offers His assessment on His path and how it will work for you; He was actually the first to fight – the first to live these challenges, overcome obstacles and show, by example, how we should live as Christians. When Jesus tells you to leave something alone, or to not walk a certain path – when He tells you to not feed a certain craving or to not let a certain appetite consume or control you – He speaks from experience and studied, practiced technique. Like the starting quarterback on a football team, He is the first to play the game and test the strategy, and He now imparts this wisdom onto you. He was the first to play and win – you can be next.

You can't design a system better than the author. You can't play the game better than the founder. You can play differently, but you need to have the same goal in mind, and you need to have the same team in mind. There is nothing better because Jesus, in effect, is our "captain". At times, we all think we are smarter, brighter, slicker, more determined than our "captain". Keep in mind, as is always the case in a battle – in a hard-won game, the captain fought the battles and will fight more battles before you do. There is nothing Jesus didn't experience; He was tempted in all areas of life like us. Play like the "captain", and you will win too.

Remember, the "author" and the "founder" of your faith has secured your destiny.

Winning this race called life.

I think it's healthy to view life as a game to be won – a race to tackle and finish with a personal best. Faith is trusting that Jesus is only telling you to train the best way for your own individual progress; your way may be different than others – slower than some and faster than others – with more challenges than some and fewer than others, but it is the best way for you. Faith truly is the best way to run this race called life. Again, Jesus was the first to run and he found a way to win; further, He seeks to teach us an individualized training path – a way to being our personal best.

Again, this is an ancient concept. Running was the most popular of the Olympic games. They ran it in a stadium, and folks would gather to see the competitors. The starting place was at the entranceway, and, at the opposite end was the goal, where the judge would sit, holding the prize in his hands. The eyes of the runners would remain fixed on the judge. If a runner knew he was wearing something that would slow him down, he would strip it off so that he would be fluid and faster in the race, because what that runner wanted was in the judges hands – the prize. He was running, not to beat the others who were running, but he was running his own personal best race to get his prize.

Jesus ran the race set before Him, which meant enduring the cross and handling the shame. How did He do that? He did that by keeping His eyes fixed on God. That's what faith is, it's running a personal race with your eyes on Jesus, because He holds your prize in His hands. And it doesn't matter how fast you run, or who beats you across the finish line, because in this race, it's not if you cross first, it's just that you cross. The race is not given to the swift, nor the battle to the strong but to he or she who endures to the end.

Paul said in Acts 20:24 and Acts 20: 13 – 14,

[24] However, I consider my life worth nothing to me, if only I may finish the race and complete the task the Lord Jesus has given me – the task of testifying to the gospel of God's grace[3].

[13] Brothers, I do not consider myself yet to have taken hold of it. But one thing I do: Forgetting what is behind and straining toward what is ahead, [14] I press on toward the goal to win the prize for which God has called me heavenward in Christ Jesus[4].

I am living with the founders faith, and that keeps me steady in storms and straight in crooked places, and I trust Him that what he left me to live with will work for me.

Moody Church News reports the experience of an English farmer who told a companion, while walking through his fields one day, "You know, I was saved by my good looks." To his surprised friend, he explained further that some time before he had attended a gospel meeting, held in his own barn. This is what happened.

Look to Jesus, Ya'll, and you can live in this world by faith.

"The preacher gave out as his first text, Isaiah 45:22: "Look unto Me, and be ye saved, all the ends of the earth: for I am God, and there is none else." He pictured the cruel cross and Jesus bearing the sin of the world. Sitting there I gazed at the amazing sight and with my inner eyes of the soul I SAW HIM DYING FOR ME.

"Then the preacher turned to a second verse, Hebrews 12:2; "Looking unto Jesus the author and finisher of our faith; who for the joy that was set before Him endured the cross, despising the shame, and is set down at the right hand of the throne of God." He pictured a Risen Savior, able to save to the uttermost all that come unto Him … able to keep us from stumbling … able to present us faultless before His throne … able to empower us to live victoriously. Somehow the sight of the mighty risen Lord Jesus showed me that **He could do the job not only for Me**, on the cross, but in me day by day.

And it doesn't matter how fast you run, or who beats you across the finish line, because in this race, it's not if you cross first, it's just that you cross.

"Then, before the preacher closed, he gave one more wonderful verse, in Titus 2:13: "Looking for that Blessed hope, and the glorious appearing of the great God and our Savior Jesus Christ." What a thrill it was to hear that this same Jesus **actually is coming again for His own blood-bought people**. So, I am looking forward to the time when I shall be with Him."

The farmer's friend was impressed. "That's wonderful! I now understand how you were saved by your good looks!"[5]

Endnotes

1 *Libronix Electronic Bible Software*

2 *Libronix Electronic Bible Software*

3 *The Holy Bible: New International Version. 1996, c1984. Zondervan: Grand Rapids*

4 *The Holy Bible: New International Version. 1996, c1984. Zondervan: Grand Rapids*

5 *Tan, P. L. 1996, c1979. Encyclopedia of 7700 illustrations: [a treasury of illustrations, anecdotes, facts and quotations for pastors, teachers and Christian workers]. Bible Communications: Garland TX*

Chapter 3: *Increase My Faith*

We've all done it – envied another or even hurt another through guidance or gesture. No matter what you tell yourself – "I have a lot" – "I am blessed" – "I have the love of my family and the prosperity of a life of hard work" it will often creep in – that feeling that we deserve more – that someone else has what we want or need. Similarly, we've all felt wronged or hurt – even attacked – or worse, led astray. Sometimes, we take it upon ourselves to make that offender – that other person – "suffer." Sometimes, we push our sense of justice too far, and we hurt others by our own actions. Often, we think we are seeking retribution. Often, we tell ourselves that it is justified. Usually, we are wrong. How do we know when to exert tolerance and when to act on a true act of hostility? Is it only when we help others? Do we always need to exercise restraint – faithfully sticking to and not straying from our own path? And, when do we forgive? Forget?

Repeat offenders; handling those who rebuff extensions of good will.

The disciples, as humble men and followers, often had questions for Jesus. The Bible does tell us that, many times, they did question motives and how to behave in certain situations. As men who were only human, they were both baffled and intrigued when they asked if they should have to forgive people who offended or hurt them and were told simply, "yes." This caused them to ask the Lord to increase their faith. The disciples, making this request of Jesus, to "increase our faith," came in the immediate aftermath of hearing Jesus talk about forgiveness, particularly forgiving someone who continues to violate the human grace extended to them.

In Luke 17:1-5 Jesus opens acknowledging that the temptations and distractions that cause us to sin will always be around. While you are in the world, you will always wrestle with things in life that will cause you to sin. Jesus suggests, however, that what you don't want to be is a person whose life and language causes other people to sin. Jesus says you would rather do severe damage to yourself than to be the cause of someone else's sin. To describe this, Jesus uses a metaphor of his own times. He says it would be better that a stone be tied around your neck and you be thrust into the sea where that stone would sink you to your own demise than to cause someone else to sin[1].

What a measure of communal accountability He gives us. That our aggressive pre-disposition should be subdued in order to encourage one another's strengths and to so desire each other's holiness above our own that we would be moved to hurt ourselves rather than to hurt someone else or cause someone else to stumble in his or her pilgrimage. This sounds like quite a bit to ask – that we should hurt ourselves before we cause another pain or to stumble in his or her quest for a faithful and chaste life. It is within our realm, however. With this rule, Jesus also sets forth a description of forgiveness and the kind of spiritual tolerance we should have for one another if we have experienced sin or hostility. He says – if your brother sins against you, you should go to him and rebuke him, which simply means to correct him. If he repents, then forgive him or treat him like he never offended you in the first place. In fact, if he offends you seven times in a day, which means he completely takes advantage of your forgiving embrace and demonstrates a total disregard for your patience and tolerance, and he repents, then forgive him every single time. The issue is never your justice or retribution but the offender's conversion.

When the disciples hear this, they respond with, " Lord, increase our faith". Why do they say this? They have listened to Jesus, and they know what He says – that they should respond to injury inflicted upon them, and they should respond to the person who inflicted it – albeit with humility, guidance and tolerance. The disciples heard this, as we do now, and they know, as we do, that this is not at all the end they would have come to given the opportunity to handle the same situation themselves. Most of us – the disciples too – know that we would initially want some sort of retribution.

They ask Jesus to increase their faith because there's a difference between how Jesus expects them to respond and how they would have actually responded. They knew that, at some point, after the first offense, the extension of their grace would have worn thin and revenge and retribution and punitive response would have been embraced and enacted. They knew that forgiving someone who then changes and never does it again is one thing, but forgiving someone who keeps doing the same thing and makes one feel unfairly victimized is quite another. The disciples are thinking about this while they are hearing Jesus, and they know they are nowhere near the place that Jesus expects them to be and so they admit it in question and confession – We are not yet capable of this, Lord; please increase our faith![2]

How often do we seek "justice"?

We all understand the disciples and their dilemma, don't we? The way we want to respond to people and to life with its swift changing climates and conditions and its subtle and, often, frustrating twists and turns is not the way God would expect, at times. This is maddening, isn't it?

We want to absorb surprises and disappointments – for us – for our children – in a way that makes us proud of our own righteousness. We want to respond to temptation in a way that makes it clear how much we love and honor God. We want to treat people who offend us in a way that others know that the grace of God is at work in our lives. We want to handle circumstances in a way that won't result in shame for what we have done or said. And we, like the disciples, have to admit that forgiving the offender once, yes, is fine, but seven times – well... that's not always "fine"! Do we ask, in these times, "Lord, I need you to increase my faith" because I am not able to do this – I cannot see the other side of this – I don't believe that things are going to get better – and even, this doesn't feel right to me? Or do we, in fact, do what does feel right or appropriate at the time often out of anger or sadness and seek revenge or retribution, even knowing that such action will, ultimately, destroy us? Further, do we ever ask for our faith to be increased when we hear what it takes to meet God's standards in certain situations and when we think about how we would respond versus what God expects of us? Truthfully, most of the time, we are not there. We need to remember to ask, "Lord please increase our faith".

Jesus, the teacher, presents to the disciples what it takes to increase their faith, thereby leaving us with lessons to help us "increase our faith".

Jesus says trust that the faith you have is enough. The evidence of any faith is the confirmation that you have enough faith to address your life's issues. Further, he says if you have faith the size of a grain of mustard seed[3], You can tell the mountain to be cast into the sea[4]. Here is the lesson. Your faith doesn't need to vary depending on the size of your challenge; you just need to apply your faith the same for big or small challenges that will come into your life. This is actually an easy premise.

Your faith doesn't need to vary depending on the size of your challenge; you just need to apply your faith the same for big or small challenges that will come into your life.

Does the size of the obstacle matter to faith?

When you live thinking your faith needs to vary depending on the size of your obstacles, you have been letting your obstacles take the lead on your measure of trust in God. Let me explain it this way. When David goes down to the battlefield on a mission to take his brothers lunch at his father's request, he has no idea he will be facing Goliath. He only makes the determination once down there after seeing how his brothers and the Israelite Army is shaking in front of this giant, Goliath. David volunteers to fight him, and he doesn't have to go somewhere and find increased faith and trust in God to handle this battle; he simply draws on the faith he uses daily as well as the fortitude he used to fight the lion and the bear. We know this because he says, in essence, you (Goliath) are bigger than they were, but I defeated them the same way I am going to defeat you. He tells Goliath (and really believes it) "the Lord is going to give you over into my hands". [5]

Our lesson? You cannot change the size of your faith to be proportionate to the level of your struggle; you are living with faith and the trust you carry and the confidence you carry in God is enough to handle whatever comes your way. That's right – whatever comes your way. You need to trust the power of your faith and trust that whatever faith you have is enough to face something as challenging as a Goliath, because as Jesus says in Luke 17:6, "You only need faith the size of a mustard seed".

Consider the Mulberry tree story in Luke 17; the tree is deeply rooted, tall in stature, secure in place and yet it will move if you trust God enough for it to move. Think hard. Is there something that has settled into your life that is intimidating you and preventing you from positive movement? Is it so impressive that you have convinced yourself that moving past it exceeds the faith you have to do so? Go ahead, apply the faith you do have to it and watch that faith deal with the enormity of your opposition, no matter how large. You do have enough faith. Activate it – rest in it – use it – believe it – and believe in it. It is enough to uproot the deepest of pain, pressure, depression, and a host of other issues.

You cannot change the size of your faith to be

proportionate to the level of your struggle

Remember, you do have the faith to rise above and forgive the offender no matter how many times you have been offended. You don't need more faith; you simply need to have trust in the faith you carry. You don't need to have another year of theological study on ethics or have a scholar's view of war and violence. You have a belief that God is real. You don't know all God's character traits or His names, but you know He is real. And Jesus is saying, while you are en route to greater revelation about God, that you have enough belief in Him to address these enormous challenges you are facing. You don't need more; you need to apply it. You don't need to know everything about Him; you can be confident in the fact that you know Him.

Make Jesus' standard your norm.

What I'm discussing regarding forgiveness sounds abnormal to us right now because culture has redefined behavioral patterns and norms so that basic human standards for love and forgiveness have decreased. In this context, it is abnormal to consider forgiving someone seven times in one day for the same offense. To us, most times, this person has become a repeat offender in our lives. By our standards as reasonable people, this is intolerable – needs to be punished – taught a lesson. What Jesus is suggesting is the opposite. Don't think of these incidents as isolated, but as a way to respond all the time – as a Christian – as a member of society. Forgiveness should be your norm.

Endnotes

1 Luke 17:2

2 Luke 17:5

3 Luke 17:6

4 Mathew 21:21

5 I Sam 17:46

Section 2

Defining Faith

Chapter 4: *Faith That Pleases God*

We tell ourselves everyday that we do walk with
God – that we love Him and try to please Him daily.
Do we walk with Him in every aspect of our lives,
however? Do we seek to bring others closer to our
union with Him – to bring them into our lives and
our fellowship with God? Think about it. Do you
always listen to your teenager when he or she wants
to talk? You may not be interested in who likes who
or who wore what, but… they need you to bring
your love to their lives – to everything that you do.
Do we keep and maintain friendships – sending that
card across miles when we don't see the friendly face
everyday – asking that person who spends a lot of
time alone to dinner… to commune with those who
love him or her? We should. These things please
others, and they please God.

The Mystery of Enoch's Walk with God

We are introduced to Enoch in Genesis chapter 5:21, as the writer of Israel's history attempts to give to us the central conflicts, similarities and personality traits that existed in and between Adam and Noah. What I find interesting is that, in each case, we are told the patriarch's name, the number of years he lived before having children, the number of sons he had, and how old he was when he died. However, when we get to verse 21, we are introduced to Enoch, who we discover lived 65 years before he became a father to a son, and then follows an unusual descriptor in that it is written, "Enoch walked with God for 300 years." Then in verse 24, we find that Enoch walked with God, then he was no more because God took him away.

Enoch's walk set him apart because of the **faith** that influenced his walk. Enoch had faith that distinguished him among those generations before him and generations after him. His faith is described as a **walk with God**. And we know it affected how he lived, but the writer of Hebrews wants us also to know that it affected how he transitioned from life temporal to life eternal. It is suggested that he did not die, but that God took him, and it was understood that this meant that God literally walked him across the chasm that separates life on this side from life on the other side.

Legends gathered around Enoch, because of the bizarre way he exited this world. You become accustomed to having a person around when they live to ages like he did, 365 years. In one instance, Enoch is spotted doing what was a part of his normal custom or routine and the next Enoch is gone, his body not found, no sightings recorded. And the legends began to swirl. Some said he was the first to be skilled in tailoring and sewing, teaching men how to cut out skins, to make their garments. Others said he was first to teach men to make shoes to protect their feet and the first to put pen to paper and instruct men from books.

Many believed that Enoch walked so close with God that he asked God one day to see into paradise, because he wanted to see what the blessed enjoy. God answered his prayer and when Enoch saw paradise, he never came back to Earth again. Some suggested that God took Enoch because of how wicked the world was and he didn't want him to be surrounded by wickedness. In essence, God may have been protecting a man who worked hard to nurture his walk with God, making such a relationship a priority.

Isn't it interesting to think that if the world was so wicked and faith so anemically present, that not one legend, myth or story suggested that Enoch slipped into curiosity or flirtation with the wicked activity of the world at that time? If wickedness prevailed, why, then, would the legend suggest that Enoch had taken the path of the faithful or reaped the reward of the faithful? No matter the legend, the myth, the story, true, conjured or otherwise, it was clear that whatever happened, God was involved and it was because of how Enoch walked with God that Enoch was chosen or involved.

We now know the peculiar nature of Enoch's life. We know that he was different than those he was around; he walked with God for more than 300 years. His walk was so distinguished that his transition from life temporal was different than everyone else around him. We are then given, in these verses, the interpretation God had of Enoch's life.

"He took him

And it pleased God"

How do we "walk with God" in our own lives?

From this, we are to glean the practical application for our own lives and that is, plainly, that what pleased God was Enoch's **faith** and that, without that kind of faith, it is impossible to please God. In fact, those that would attempt to live life like this must first believe that God is all-powerful and loving, and that He is, in fact, a "rewarder" of those who diligently seek Him.

We have already established that faith for us is obedient trust in the word of God despite our circumstances or conditions. And, quite simply, the story of Enoch supports that notion that our faith must be a faith that seeks to walk with God.

This is challenging because we come to God through a faith that we are taught responds to God. We are told that we don't seek him; we are told that, in fact, we are saved because He seeks us. Paul says that we have gone from dead[2] in trespasses and sins, to made alive in Christ Jesus. Our minds were blind and unable to see the gospel, but God took the initiative and shaped our lives to hear His word and receive His invitation to an intimate relationship with Him. When He found us, we responded with belief and confession and, for many, our faith stays in that posture. We know that God "is", and we know that He requires certain things of us. We know him to be good, and to bless us, and we worship to stay sensitive to His voice and welcoming of His presence. We do those things that please Him because we want to keep receiving blessings as He has promised He will give to those who stay faithful to Him.

For the most part, if God wants to change something in us, all He has to do is let us know, right? If He wants us to go in another direction, we just need the signals, don't we? How many times do we ask for signs – closed doors, lightening bolts, a single word whispered in our ear. We say, "Let something clearly reveal Your intentions, God, and I will obediently respond. If He wants us to be active in ministry, we say "no problem, God, just catch us as we live and tell us what You want us to do." We gladly say, "You got it, God, because I am grateful for who You are and for what You do."

Many of us shape our spiritual lives this way, and, in the story of Enoch, we are challenged to consider that faith as it grows doesn't just operate by pushing you to respond to God, it will push you beyond being sought and into the realm of seeker. In the interpretation of Enoch's walk with God, it is apparent that Enoch sought God in belief, and diligently so. His faith was no longer just at the point where he was readily responsive to what God wanted to bring to his life, but his faith had moved to a place where he was passionately pursuing God and God was so pleased with that – that He walked Enoch across the chasm of death.

Truly living your faith.

So, we need to consider, is our faith only responsive to the presence of God, or is our faith actively pursuing God. In fact, are you addressing areas of your life because God is on your back and you feel obligated to have faith in Him or are you addressing areas of your life because you want to be so close to God that you are tired of living in a way that keeps you from achieving your goals? Is God removing those things from your life that currently hinder your spiritual walk, or are you freely giving up to Him those things that hinder your spiritual walk?

What's the angle here? There is a difference in having a level of faith that is responsive to God as opposed to one that is proactive in service to God and faith. Do you hear Him when He talks? Do you move when He prompts you to? Most of us attempt to obey when He shows us the need for change. However, that is only one dimension of faith, and there must be another dimension of faith, specifically the process of actively seeking God for closer inspection of our spiritual lives. In other words, we need to seek Him instead of waiting for Him to find us. So, dig deep and ask yourself: Am I pursuing Him when I need to make a decision or when I lack guidance? Or, do I do more than that? One way to describe it in terms that reflect our busy, modern lives is to picture a world in which God speaks to us by cell phone. You have His number; He has yours. When He calls, you ignore His call and never call Him back, yet, when you call Him, He always answers. We all need to begin initiating calls to God, unsolicited, for no reason – just to say "hi" and to express our faith. This is precisely the kind of faith that Enoch had; God didn't have to call Enoch because whenever he thought about dialing his number,

God's cell phone was already ringing and Enoch's name was appearing on the caller ID.

The next level of faith.

This is your next level of faith. You have developed a faith that responds to God's presence, and now God wants you to exercise a faith that chases God's presence. You have a faith that can hear His voice and when He speaks you know its Him; He wants you to exercise a faith that asks Him to speak even if its not about something particularly relevant to your life. He wants to know that you have a relationship with Him – a respect – a dialogue.

Think about it. How hungry or desperate are you for what God has to offer? Are you only as desperate as one who will be ready when the Lord is ready to move, or are you so hungry that you are pounding on heaven's doors asking whether it is time to meet your fate – time to fulfill your destiny? You need to be ready to pound on the doors of heaven in order to please God.

Doesn't Enoch's story really illustrate the fellowship of faith? Enoch walked with God. For him, it wasn't spirituality as a discipline but spirituality as a lifestyle. He didn't just have a relationship with God to simply enhance his relationship with other people; for Enoch, his primary goal was his relationship with God and every other interaction stemmed from that. There is a big difference between the two types of relationships. We need to understand that.

Can we expect God to decide whether He can be God to you with the decisions you make and the places you deem purposeful and the people to whom you connect your destiny? Or do you take the initiative and shape everything in your life in terms of their importance to your relationship with God? Do you base your decisions and your lifestyle upon who God is to you first because your fellowship with Him is more important than anything else? These are all points to consider.

I was thinking about all this the other day after picking my daughter up from school. We were in the car, just laughing and having a good time – one of those "laugh so hard you tear up" kind of afternoons. There was nothing really important making us laugh; we were just laughing because we were together and life was good, and the day was drawing to a close, and… it had been a nice day. I thought – this is great, but when the laughter stops, I sure hope that someday, she will be mature enough to understand that just asking me to accept who she dates and spends her time with is not enough, but that demanding an understanding from all those she chooses to allow into her life is an understanding of the importance of the fellowship the two of us share. I do want her to evaluate her friends based on the strength of my fellowship with her. I don't want to smother her, and I have never parented before – in fact, I'm learning as I go, but… I do want her to evaluate her relationships by whether or not these people could grow a fellowship with me and with her and respect what we currently have and build on that.

Faith pursues fellowship with God.

If this is true, and your faith will allow you to pursue fellowship with God, then everything else in your life will have to find existence in that fellowship. In other words, to know you is to know the God you walk with: To want you is to want the God you walk with. You need to understand, as do the people in your life, that there is NO greater pursuit than the pursuit of God's fellowship in your life.

Now we understand the fellowship of faith, but we need to examine the focus of that fellowship, the focus of faith. Part of focusing on faith is diligently doing so, diligently seeking God. The word "diligent" means to constantly go after what one is going after, and in our case, we need to make it our walk with God. In this case, in attempting a successful walk with God, we need to always be investigating the value and strength of our diligent pursuit of God and make it priority to be successful.

It's risky, but if you are on the cusp of believing that God is real and that God is worth surrendering your life to, investigate it, look around, and examine the competition for what you want to influence your life. When you look at all your other options, and... when it comes to the decisions you need to make and the moves you are contemplating as well as the people who want space in and influence over your life, make sure you are truly investigating it all deeply. Once you do this type of introspective search, certainly, your fellowship with God will remain the best thing that could have ever happened in your life. God will come out the winner in any competition.

We need to always be investigating the value and strength of our diligent pursuit of God and make it priority to be successful.

Rewards for the Seeker

In the story of Enoch, we see that he looked at all the wickedness that was taking place around him, and he determined that there was NOTHING better than his fellowship with God and he pursued it. He chased after it until he is described as having "walked with God".

To use Enoch as an example means that your focus in life would be, first, to walk with God, knowing that everything else would fall into place. This, of course, creates anxiety because there is so much in life we want, and we know that we should have an urgency about certain things such as a house big enough to make our family comfortable, a job that sustains our lifestyle, positive relationships that make us happy. The evidence here suggests, however, that if you seek God, like Enoch, you will be rewarded as a diligent seeker, also as Enoch was. In fact, when it came time for Enoch to walk through death like every other man, his faith was so strong in God, and he had walked with God so passionately, that God walked with him across what everyone else must walk through alone.

Everyone else had to taste death, and then be translated to eternal life, but not Enoch; he walked with God, and his fellowship with God was so strong that he was walked across safely, happily from this life to the next – paradise. What if his fellowship had not been that strong? Would he walk alone? Would he see paradise?

Whatever you're going through – whatever stress or strain is giving you cause for worry now – know that you can walk with God and enjoy your fellowship with Him – even reap the rewards of that fellowship in your daily life and still walk to paradise with God when this life is over. Try to understand that you may have to face things that others don't or you may have to get through difficult times that seem hard to bear, but... trust in your fellowship with God, and He will lead you to paradise – to your reward. If you please God, rest assured, you can change what will happen. If you please God, you can get through the difficult times. If you please God, you can have rewards, which will far exceed the earthly constraints of pay and wages. If you please God, you can attain that which you seek. Be like Enoch and others driven to fellowship with God, become driven to work for Him, and then reap your eternal reward.

John Wesley[3] averaged three sermons a day for 54 years, preaching more than forty four thousand times, traveling more than two hundred thousand miles by horseback to preach the gospel. He would get up at four in the morning and work till ten at night, taking breaks only to eat and yet he said he had more private time than any man in England. At 83, he was piqued to discover that he could not write more than 15 hours a day without hurting his eyes, and, at age 86, he was ashamed because he could only preach twice a day. In his 86th year of living, he was still traveling between 30 to 50 miles just to preach the gospel.

What made him preach like that and press like that? I will tell you what it was; he walked with God, and he wanted constant fellowship with God. Some of you are driven like that too; you just want to be closer to God, to hear His word, to feel His presence, to enjoy His holiness, to be changed by His word, and to know His will. It is what rewards you everyday and allows you to enjoy your life and administer to others. This is the reward of the seeker's faith:

- Love God.

- Understand God.

- Look for God.

- Nurture your relationship with God.

- Walk for God.

Endnotes

1 Hebrews 11:5

2 Ephesians 2:1-5

3 John Wesley the Methodist: A Plain Account of his life and work, John Fletcher Hurst, 1903.

Chapter 5: *Faith That Builds*

*In living a chaste and humble life, one that is
filled with love for others, duty to community, and
responsibility for our own actions, it is often difficult
to make sense of daily attacks on our sense of what
is right, what is good, what we should be doing.
Obstacles exist – people with hidden agendas at work,
cruel bullies at school, and harried, misdirected people
in all areas of our lives – at the grocery store, the dry
cleaners, even at church or at the doctor's office. It
is, therefore, even more difficult when it appears that
all sorts of other influences – in politics, the media,
and even in our neighborhoods. There is the easy
attempt to sway us from our path in life – the path of
the faithful. It is difficult to build faith when our faith
is so consistently attacked, but it is not impossible;
though, it does require some strength and focus.*

Jude and the Libertines

Jude is writing to those who are being called on to defend their faith in a climate saturated by what some theologians called Libertines. These were people, who denied the lordship of Jesus, who were not afraid to defend their beliefs. The Libertines were also extremely sexually promiscuous. Jude communicates that he is worried because those to whom he is writing and administering are being attacked and possibly influenced by the cultural promiscuity and other immoral behavior prevalent during that time. He also worries that they are not strong enough to defend the faith without becoming distracted or converted by the practices that are so prevalent around them.

As a result, Jude attempts to train the saints to defend the faith. His admonishment of the current immorality surrounding them is clear, and it is obvious that his admonishment of such hedonism helps the chaste and pure stay strong against faith's attacks.

Jude is aware that a vulnerable Christian is one whose faith is weak or infantile even though he or she might feel strong in that faith. We spend a lot of time talking about how to develop faith in terms of attaching ourselves to the seed of faith. The Bible says in Romans 10:17, that "faith comes to us by hearing the word of God from one called and sent to preach that word". Is it safe to suggest, however, that we have, at times, a faith that believes in Jesus, but not a faith to fight against what pulls us from the center of God's will or keeps us satisfied walking upon the narrow road of spiritual righteousness? I know God is real; most of us feel our faith is at least at that point, but our faith may not yet be at a place in which turning down certain temptations with a strong "not interested" is prevalent. Our faith might be strong enough to believe God for what He promised, but it's not strong enough to help us overcome some strong contrary or negative issues in our lives. We have faith, but what do we do to strengthen it to make a difference regarding some of these very difficult issues in our lives?

Jude suggests that you have to build yourself up in your faith. Many of us have developed *a* faith but not *developed* faith. Jude says you would be strong and steady if you weren't being attacked like you are, but since the attack is so strong, you need to be fortified in your faith. The stronger the attacks, the harder your obstacles, and the greater your resistance – the harder your trials, the more grueling your course, and the greater your pressure – the more demanding your ministry, resulting in the need for a faith that builds you.

> *Many of us have developed a faith*
>
> *but not developed faith.*

The Fight.

I'm a boxing fan and recently watched a pretty intense fight between two professionals. One had enjoyed a huge, successful career – the other was a newer fighter and tough, but… not quite as seasoned. It was clear, however, that this newer fighter was out for blood and, the seasoned veteran seemed to realize that. It got me thinking as I watched. This fight is demanding. I'm sure this veteran fighter has had some fights that did not demand as much or threaten his position as much as this fight with the hungry newcomer. He could train moderately for lesser opponents, but the size and strength and skill of his most recent foe demanded that he come to the ring in better shape, with greater skill and that he be more focused than ever before. And he couldn't buy what he needed to win that fight; he had to build it, through training and adding on to the skills he already had – he had to build up his boxing arsenal to be the one victoriously standing when the final bell rang. You need to do this; we all need to do this. Jude tells the saints that to defend their faith they will need to build themselves *in* faith.

We don't need some great, new revelation, or some super deliverance or some big kingdom break because what we are facing and fighting is not going away. The threat of this pull from faith – the constant presence of the temptation – the memory of what tries to entice you – is not going away. But that doesn't mean you have to suffer because of it or slow the pace of your journey. What it does mean is that you have to build yourself up in your faith – become stronger – fortify that arsenal; then, and only then, will you be able to define what is spiritually important to you.

Building faith on a foundation.

You have to build faith. What, exactly, does Jude mean by that? Build in this case comes from a word that when translated means – "to create something new or to construct anything new"[1]. Most of what you are fighting and facing doesn't need fortification from some new construct – some new source. We all need to "build upon" the foundation we already have. Jude suggests that you finish the structure on which the foundation has already been laid.

So – that brings us to our next question; what are we building upon? Is it the belief we have that God is real, and that He rewards those who diligently seek Him? If we don't face what torments us, we are still debating whether or not God can get us through any difficult times. If we establish that foundation – that we know God will prevail – we can build upon that to feel the confirmation that God is going to work on our behalf to bring our victories to pass.

Maybe we already believe this, but maybe your question is how, exactly, do I build myself up in my faith?

The Strength of the Holy Spirit

Jude says we build our faith by praying in the Holy Spirit. Now, simply defined, this means to make prayers – or to offer prayers to God. That fact is simple; however, how we pray here is not so easily understood. Your prayer, in this context, is active prayer – aggressive prayer. You need to actively offer prayers to God through the Spirit. In fact, this is the first action you need to take to build yourself up in your faith – to reach for God in the Spirit.

So remember, you need to build yourself up because you're prone to weaken and become susceptible to the dominant influence of those who would pull you from your faith. Your faith is present but not always strong enough to withstand temptation. You have to build upon what you know – fortify that inherent knowledge and strength. You know, for sure, that you can trust God, and you know that you believe He's real. Jude suggests this is a good place to start – to start building that faith. Stay vigilant, however; since you know that without faith you are not strong enough to stay your course – if you're not active enough to show your desire for a stronger faith, you may not be able to walk away from the lure of worldly temptation. And here, is where the devil moves in – where he focuses. If the enemy can keep you focused on the frailty of your humanity absent the power of God's spirit, you will anchor there in regret and disappointment. You can't let this happen. Focus on your strength.

Truth and your quest for a stronger faith.

Tell the truth about where you are in your quest to build and strengthen your faith. Realize or admit that you are not strong enough to resist or filled enough to not want what isn't good for you. Also, remember that you do have the foundation enough to know what your first action ought to be and that's to pray about it and let God direct you. Do not lose sight of that.

"Keep yourselves in God's love as you wait."[2]. Watch and be careful to stay in God's love while you wait. The metaphor is of a warden who guards prisoners against escape. The suggestion here is, while you are building your faith, guard yourself, knowing you will, if not watched closely, stray and ruin the life that you have. Pay attention to what's around you. You will then know when you are trying to make a dangerous break with faith when you attach to something other than the love of God.

When you stop speaking about yourself or others based upon the word of God, Jude says watch carefully, then guard yourself, but… with what? With God's love, of course. This much we've discussed. Feel free to live with your decisions and explore your options but do so all in the love of God. He loves you too much; don't allow life to shape you apart from the destiny God has for you, instead fight to be faithful to the providential will of God concerning your life.

Picture this. There is a single mother who can't pay her rent. Her children are in need, and she wants to provide for them. She has tried the best she can. She is feeling bad – scared – insecure and judged. Without looking, she comes into contact with a predator, who creeps in when he senses her faith is waning, someone who wants personal carnal fulfillment. He promises to pay her rent. She struggles with what to do. And we know, don't we? Her decision will be based upon where she chooses to draw her strength and her influence. If she listens to her financial condition, her children crying and maybe some of her eager, misdirected friends, she may say "yes" – and let him have his way. If she builds herself up in the love of God, she says to herself, God loves me too much to have me compromise myself to get my rent paid – or dehumanized to have some security. When she takes her actions and her faith-based decisions to the throne of God, God will say, "because you were willing to wait on Me, I will make all the happiness you want, need and deserve – finally yours."

"They that wait upon the Lord shall renew their strength."[3]

Stop talking defeated. Stop accepting mediocrity. Stop telling yourself what you cannot do. Build yourself up in your faith by taking your concerns to the Lord and letting His love motivate you. A hymn writer says, "I was sinking deep in sin, far from the peaceful shore, very deeply stained within – sinking to rise no more, but … the master of the sea heard my despairing cry and from the waters lifted me. Now, safe am I." How did you get lifted? He was asked. "Love lifted me. When nothing else could help, it was God's love that lifted me."[4]

We all need to lift ourselves in faith. Remember to:

- Stay focused.

- Remain true to faithful influences.

- Not let the easy path sway you from your mission in Christ.

- Trust in God and His love for you.

- Focus on your strength.

- Become the best God wants you to be.

Endnotes

1 Libronix Electronic Bible Software

2 Jude verse 22

3 Isaiah 40:31

4 New National Baptist Hymnal, Triad Publications, 1977.

Chapter 6: *Faith That Protects*

Have you ever been so tested that you feel like you might compromise your own belief system so that it's no longer recognizable to even you – just to belong – just to please others? Have you ever been hurt to the point of tears because your conviction in something or even just your interests were so judged and scrutinized that it made you feel you had done something wrong? It is hard to stick to your beliefs sometimes. It is hard to ignore the jeers and nasty comments from others. And worse, it is often frightening to think that you might be punished or hurt for your beliefs – the beliefs that you hold very sacred.

Peter and the "strangers".

In I Peter, Peter writes to Saints who, because of their relationship to Christ have become strange or mysterious to those in the world. These strangers, as they are called, have beliefs that have elevated them above the temporal and carnal concerns of this world, and they meditate and converse about things that are spiritual and heavenly. Their hope has been expanded to envision an end that will result in eternal communion with God in a place far beyond sun, moon and stars.

How did these "strangers" get here spiritually? In plain terms, they experienced the rejuvenation of a salvation that comes with meeting and accepting Jesus Christ. Peter, therefore, refers to them as strangers because their respective lifestyles are different than those still so enmeshed in the earthly world's playground that they see these followers of Jesus as different and even abnormal.

The hope that these "strangers" have in Jesus is simply that they believe that a life in Him is the only life worth living; they sincerely believe that His word – everything He says – will come to pass and that He will deliver all His promises, right down to eternal life. They are banking on this, and it's not too difficult to do because, along the way to the ultimate fulfillment of that which is eternity in heaven, there are countless blessings and strength of fellowship with those who hold similar beliefs. And this is comforting, isn't it?

Overcoming the non-believers.

However, these strangers are not making their way to promise without opposition and some difficulties, the hardest of which is the suffering they are enduring at the cruel hands of those who consider them strange. Those who do not follow Christ don't like the lifestyle that the "strangers" preach, promote and practice, and they are making them suffer for it in every way possible. Persecution has come to these followers of Jesus because of their attachment to He who was crucified and is rumored to have been resurrected – all for the sins of man – God's son.

In reflecting on the story that Peter tells, it seems easy, doesn't it? To celebrate a trip that has no obstacles and only smooth uninterrupted passage? It's easy to make a journey that has no threats for stopping you from arriving at your destination. It's easy to have faith that is never tested or stretched or challenged or opposed. Peter speaks or writes to these strangers to encourage them because anyone's faith can get shaky when the right kind of suffering is inflicted. So… as you reflect on this – does it seem easy for these "strangers"? They have the favor of God and the love of His son, Jesus Christ. They have the joy that having such a strong conviction holds, but we should all know that which has the ability to shake our faith to its core? Didn't the "strangers" suffer to that extent? It is good to have Peter and others who care and support such strong, unusual beliefs in a world that doesn't understand them. And how often do we see that now?

Peter extends his support to them because he knows their suffering is affecting them, and he also knows that, sadly, the suffering is just beginning. They are suffering locally at the time, but Peter is well aware of the fact that they are about to feel the weight of the Roman Empire come down on them, and if they cannot handle the suffering being inflicted upon them locally, they will buckle under the weight of Roman oppression.

In his letter, Peter refers to suffering 15 times. It is on his mind; he is worried. He wants to communicate his understanding – his empathy – and issue a warning at the same time. These Christians were suffering because they were living Godly and right lives. They were suffering because people hated the name of Jesus and anybody attached to that name. It would get worse. Peter is counting on their strength.

Peter wants to do two things. He wants them to be good witnesses in their persecution.

Why? At this time, it would be very productive to convert their oppressors and, at the same time, bring glory to the name of Jesus. And he wants them to hold on to their faith. He says then what we should all believe now, don't let what you are going through make you shaky about your trust and confidence in Christ. The greatest thing you need to get through this hostility and oppression is your faith. When your faith gets shaky, things are headed downhill for sure.

Faith is your lifeline.

Faith is your connection to the Lord. Faith is your inspiration to motivate you to keep walking when you want to quit. Faith is your stability; it helps you to interpret properly what you are going through. It is your response to the suffering you are enduring. It is your mantra; your repeated conviction when you want to stand your strongest.

> *Don't let what you are going through make you shaky about your trust and confidence in Christ.*

But faith, Peter says, is the only thing that positions you for something other than what you would normally consider. Peter says you are going through this because your enemies are trying to block you from an inheritance that is yours through Christ – your inheritance of eternal life. And your faith **protects** you and shields you and guards you en route to your inheritance.

Peter, one of Christ's apostles says, plainly, "Praise be to the God and Father of our Lord Jesus Christ!" **(I Peter 1:3).** In His great mercy, He has given us new birth into a living hope through the resurrection of Jesus Christ from the dead, and into an inheritance that can never spoil or fade – kept in heaven for you. This inheritance is yours through faith; it is where you will be shielded by God's power until the coming of the salvation that is ready to be revealed.

Interesting words. I don't know how many of us have thought about this before, but our faith is more than what we use to stay connected to God. Our faith shields us against the intent to cause pain, which, in turn, protects us from real suffering. It is this with which these saints live. Your faith should protect you from the suffering that is trying to stop you from getting your inheritance, which is eternal life in the presence of God.

Most of us have been introduced to a faith that connects us to a heritage authored by Jesus himself. He is the author and finisher of our faith. We've learned that. We have studied that this faith gives us access into the grace of God, but now we look at a faith that protects us. Our trust in God shields us from certain realities intended to distract and destroy me. This we all must remember.

God's Shield

These words, "protect' or "shield", are military words that imply a guardianship. God is guarding us against what is attempting to get into our lives and destroy our personal convictions. This is something to celebrate – that when we are overwhelmed with fear or other hurdles, God shields us from the worst of it.

But let's interpret what God must be saying when He is guarding our lives and some hostility, difficulties, ridicule or pain gets through. If He is guarding our lives, then why does some "stuff" get through? When it does, rest assured:

- You're equipped to handle it.

- You are positioned to learn and grow from it.

- You cannot ignore it. The fact that He let it in means you are to pay strict attention to its presence and your response to it.

My faith has to be strong enough to accept what God lets in and what God let's get through. The whole world observed the victims of Hurricane Katrina – the pain, fear and injustice they suffered. Do we remember, though, how Hurricane Rita, in the immediate aftermath of the first storm, hit the same general area? In fact, people providing shelters for evacuees from New Orleans in Houston had to turn around and evacuate themselves. How frustrating. But did they lose faith? It may have wavered, but those people stayed strong.

Your faith should protect you from the suffering that is trying to stop you from getting your inheritance, which is eternal life in the presence of God.

What about the certain realities you face that stretch and choke and challenge your faith? There may be realities that are fatiguing you emotionally and spiritually. Why is God letting this get through when He is guarding your life? Is He not strong enough to shield us from everything? Does He have blind spots that our enemies have identified and they use to attack us when God is not looking? Can we assume that God lets certain things get through His guard because we should be at a place in which the inheritance He has for us should motivate us to put up a good fight? At that time, will He empower us so we win? Yes. We are being tested. Are you willing to fight for your inheritance? It is interesting to note, too, that what gets through may be what he knows we are capable of fighting. Our faith was tested before, and we passed. The next time, he presses us harder.

My faith has to be strong enough to accept what God lets in and what God let's get through.

Our faith protects us, but understand this: Not only is the Lord shielding us from difficulties, He is shielding the inheritance from us. He is guarding the inheritance He has for all mankind. He is guarding those trying to block you from it, but He is also guarding you against what you might be doing or allowing that would sway you from the path to your inheritance. Your faith, basically, protects you against self-sabotage. God challenges the way you think and the steps you take. He knows it's not always because the enemy is influencing you and you are spiritually dehydrated; He knows how difficult it is to discern between the voice and will of God and your own wants and desires. In other words, God has to guard you against things that look good to you but are not good for you – things that feed ego and not spirit.

Are you willing to fight for your inheritance?

Whether we want to confess it or not – face the hard facts or not – we need to acknowledge that we sure have the capacity to mess it all up, don't we? We don't need Satan's influence; he doesn't have to tempt me or attack me. My nature un-surrendered to Jesus would create a life that would cause me to forfeit my inheritance, and I need to stay on top of that – we all do. Thank God that Jesus loves us more than we love ourselves, and He protects us from that in us, which would cost us our inheritance.

Now who can't trust God in Christ to guard your life? After all this discussion, if you can't believe that God is a "rewarder" of those who diligently seek Him, you must not be feeling too rewarded right now. If you can't believe that God will open doors because your hand has only touched doors that have been closed and you can't believe that God can work miracles because nothing in your life seems to be turning around, then you must at least confess that, without a shadow of a doubt, you believe that God can protect you from what is trying to get to you. The God we serve is a loving God, a blessing God, and a God that fights for you.

We saw that in Israel.

We saw that with David. We saw that with Elijah, and if we missed those, we sure enough saw it on Calvary, in the resurrection of the Lord Jesus Christ.

Chapter 7: *Faith that Hungers*

How strong is your conviction when it comes to something that you believe is right? If you don't get positive affirmation right away, do you throw in the towel? If you were told to toil in your job for a year without pay – with the promise of greater pay – greater insights into the world – and fantastic career rewards – if you just did this one thing, toil tirelessly for one year, without pay, you would reap these rewards. Would you do it? Would you believe it? Would your hunger for more knowledge, greater safety, and even higher standing in the community entice you and sustain you while others scoffed and laughed? I think we're all capable of such a test, if we have the right mix of faith.

The Story of Noah

For 120 years, Noah was engaged in a project that thoroughly confused and amused people around him. Never before, since the creation of humanity, had the Earth flooded in such a way that one would need to build an ark the size that Noah was working on. No one around him had developed a spiritual life intimate enough with God that God would trust him with His divine intentions like God trusted Noah. What Noah is doing is God-inspired and God-fed and, further, only he sees God's intentions; in fact, he cannot find in those around him, even a small group of people that are sensitive enough to God to understand why this ark is being constructed.

Hebrews 11:7 shares Noah's commitment to work on this Ark without ever having seen rain or flood was his faith in God. By faith, Noah was instructed to build the Ark. In fact, his faith positioned him in order for God to show him what he needed to do to be ready to survive given God's next plan for humanity – a flood.

 It is exciting to think that God will feed our faith by showing us where we need to be so that we are prepared for His next move for the world. Think for a moment about the graciousness of God to ensure that those who are connected to Him in faith will not be left behind based upon what He is intending to do; the faithful will not be caught off guard. Those connected to Him will not have to guess what comes next. The faithful will know His will, His intentions and His purpose. This suggests that whatever else you want to be – spiritually strong in your witness, generous in the use of your gifts – that you will certainly want to pay attention to the presence of faith in your life, the maturity of faith in your life, and the sensitivity of your faith to the voice and will of God. If God is willing to share with you where you need to be positioned in order to live strong with what He is intending to do, it would not be logical for you to let God move and react to how God moves as opposed to positioning yourself in faith and becoming prepared for what comes next.

When I'm sick, I call the doctor and, if he's not available, I leave my number and wait for his call. I pay attention to the phone, and I wait for that call, knowing that the doctor will respond before too long. Similarly, if I want to know what God is intending to do and hear what He is willing to share, I want to keep the channel as open and as clear as I can. I am happy that faith is the place He has chosen to rest His will and His plans and His purposes. I can do faith, right? Understand, however, that the stronger your faith is, the more He can show you concerning what He intends to do with your life. The stronger your faith, the deeper the revelation God will share with you. Now, the question you must ask yourself is, can you do it? Can you stay open to faith? Can you feel a real need for it? A hunger?

> *The stronger your faith, the deeper the revelation*
> *God will share with you.*

Noah knew that he didn't need a life that only *reacted* to God's will; he needed a life that *prepared* for God's will. Can I dare suggest that what you are seeing only makes sense to you, only has your attention the way it does because others will react to it or respond to it? Can I suggest that we all might be bound by earthly desires and influences? God wants you to be more prepared for whatever may come your way, though – physically, mentally, emotionally, and, yes, spiritually.

How does God feed our faith?

God fed Noah's faith. In fact, the Bible says that, by faith, Noah was divinely warned of things not yet seen. At the time, the world was corrupt; people were becoming increasingly more distant from God, and God was determined that He would wipe humanity out and start over with a remnant of the faithful. Noah was the chosen vessel to repopulate the Earth. God shares this with Noah, and, then, proceeds to tell him everything. He tells him the specifics of the ark down to the exact measurements. He tells him what material should be used to construct it and exactly how many animals need to be secured and placed within the Ark; He even tells him how many windows and of what size and shape they should be. God tells Noah to do this because it is going to rain, and the rain is going to claim the life of every human being and living creature that walks the earth, but Noah and his family and chosen animals on the ark will be saved.

God tells Noah that the condition of humanity has become dire. Wickedness is everywhere, and the promise of the flood and the details concerning the Ark are Noah's alone – to cleanse the world. Does this mean that Noah had been asking questions about God's plan? Had he noticed the wickedness and become concerned? Was he tired of fighting such evil on his own? It is clear that Noah found refuge in God until his faith was strengthened and his mission clear.

In Hebrews 11, it is suggested that Noah built the ark because of his faith. We know that Noah had questions, and his questions made him hungry for knowledge about what God was going to do. He asked hard questions; he got hard answers. We all know that our faith does grow when we ask of God and get answers – difficult or otherwise. When we have answers, we feel empowered and we hunger for more. This is a good thing. If we were to stop asking questions, we would notice the hole that is created when we don't have the answers we need – when our hunger dies and, as a result, our faith begins to wane. We need to renew that relationship through worship and continued union with God, with Noah as our example. Worship is the laboratory for intimacy; faith is the laboratory for revelation. You want to know what God is doing, what God is up to – then you need a faith that asks questions. Have you noticed that the more your faith grows the more questions you have?

It is OK to question God.

I hope your faith is at a place where you feel you can ask questions of God about you, about others and about what He intends to do with both. You can't be a person of faith and not ask God questions such as why is the world population given to war and wicked governmental diplomacy? You can't be a person of faith and not ask how, in this post-modern world we live in, a man can get away with walking into a diner with a tee shirt with depictions of African Americans with ropes tied around their necks on it and other awful intrusions on human dignity and respect and kindness to others. This is certainly appalling. Use your faith to ask God why children are so afraid of their own futures that they have resorted to carrying guns to school or why there are so many families breaking up and why are so many people on the edge of mental collapse. You may not like the answers; His answers may ask a lot of you – almost more than you feel that you can give, but in order to bring change to the sinful nature of the world, as Noah did, you have to open yourself to God's will. Become one of the trusted – one of those filled with faith, and God will speak to you. The more you ask, the more you will understand His intentions for this world and your role in them. You will also begin to understand His plan for you.

Noah was asking these questions, and God responded to him. God knows the questions your faith is asking and He has the answer and if He hasn't revealed it to you yet, you need to keep asking the questions and keep growing your faith, because the hunger of your faith will get you the answers that you seek.

Noah's faith was hungry. Hungry to know, hungry to be prepared, and hungry to be used for God's will. Does your faith show God how much you want to know about what He is up to? Does your faith show God how much you want to be prepared for what God is going to do in you and in the world? Does your faith demonstrate to God how desperate you are to live obedient to Him? Think about it, and ask yourself the ultimate question: How do I live like this?

Develop a faith that questions.

Don't ask the wrong questions. Don't ask the wrong people.
Stop looking for faith in all the wrong places. Above all, do not
feel like you only need to respond to God. Instead, develop an
attitude for questioning what is expected of you. Don't fall prey
to the wickedness of the world by ignoring what it going on
around you. Diligently seek God. Diligently question him, and
answer the call to help. Do what He tells you to do. Revel in the
fact that He has shared with you His intentions for a world gone
wrong – for a society in need of help. Offer that help; accept the
challenge. If you remain open to this, you are one of the faithful.

Trust that God's Word can be believed and obeyed and followed.
In this way, your faith will become the lens through which you
see life and through which you evaluate life. You don't look at
life the same way when you don't know Jesus; you need to know
Him intimately. You will see with a spiritual eye, which will force
you to ask some different questions – deeper questions. What
does God want me to do with the life I have been given?
Not, why didn't I get that job or why don't I have more money?
Faith creates a deeper evaluation and action.

Trust that God's Word can be believed

and obeyed and followed.

Faith and Prayer

The premise is simple. You will not get the right answers asking
the wrong questions, and you will not get the right answers
asking the right questions of the wrong person. Noah had faith
that raised questions, and he had faith in God. He trusted God
with the most important questions in the world: What will
happen to me and what will happen to humanity? Beyond that,
how can I help? What do You ask of me? Ask yourself. Have your
questions, in prayer or otherwise, been shaped by your emotions,
your circumstances, other people, modern ethics and not your

faith in God? If so, you need to go back and nurture a faith that shapes questions only worthy of answers from God, and then, poise your life to hear His answers. I promise you, God will show you that the flood is coming and when you need that ark to survive it. This is all good news.

What does God want me to do with the life

I have been given?

How do you live with this kind of faith?

First, develop a faith that questions. Second, discipline a faith to be fed by reverence not evidence. Third, respect your God; understand that He knows best. You asked – now listen.

Think about Noah and how hard it was for him to build that ark. There was no one supporting him. Everyone laughed at him and ridiculed him. There was much hard work ahead of him. Anyone can see how difficult it was for Noah to build the ark. We have all seen storms and floods, hurricanes and tsunamis. We have witnessed the devastation. History will certainly record that one of the most devastating hurricanes of our generation was Katrina, which wiped New Orleans out, and we are watching them return at a snail's pace to something that resembles a city. How can you rebuild the city for the sake of tourism when the original residents of the city can't even live there? We know that in most northern cities, as winter approaches and weather reports indicate a major storm is coming our way, we need to take the reports seriously. We stock up on supplies and make preparations for the storm's severity. We react instantly because we have seen what damage the storm can do and not being prepared can have dire consequences. Are we prepared for other such storms in life?

Now, Noah had never seen a flood. Yet, he was instructed to build an ark for a storm he couldn't even fathom. Not only has he never seen it, but no one around him has ever seen it either. And Noah has to listen to his critics over 120 years, critics who are constantly chiding him, especially since it doesn't seem possible that a storm or a flood is on the way. Talk about conviction. How many times do you think he was told he was wrong? How many people have withdrawn fellowship from him because he persisted in moving forward in faith when the skies were clear and the ground was dry? How many days has he doubted his own movements? And yet he built that ark in obedience, didn't he?

He built it because he stands too in awe of God to doubt God. That's what reverence means. This is healthy awe or fear of God. It makes you, for example, straighten up when you enter the sanctuary and no matter how great your life might be – when you come to church, you want to dress up and demonstrate your best behavior. This is healthy awe and what I am suggesting is this: You don't nurture a hungry faith on evidence; instead, feed a hungry faith on reverence.

If you need evidence of some of what God is going to do in your life, then your faith needs to grow. You shouldn't need evidence if you have true faith. Trust His will. Trust His faith in you. God wants to show you His will, but He wants you to accept it on reverence alone. Do you love Him enough to know its going to rain, if not today maybe tomorrow, maybe 120 years from now? You should.

Feed this faith.

This kind of faith will discipline you to ignore what people are saying. No one around you can tell you what God is showing just you. They can't interpret it; they can't make sense out of it. People ask me all the time to help them interpret dreams, and I am quick to say this: That I do believe that God speaks through dreams, but I do not have the gift of interpreting them. I would advise that you not talk to anyone but God about them, because if God had something to tell you that required a deposit in a private dream, it is serious and it is for you alone. Begin to discern the importance of what He is telling you. Begin to give Him your important questions. Don't be afraid to ask Him what He intends for you or for mankind.

It is understandable to try and humanize what God tells us. As humans, we need support. We need people who affirm. We need people to agree. This is in our nature. Keep in mind: If Noah needed affirmation and support from people, he would have never built the ark or completed it; in fact, he had to work on the ark when it wasn't popular and wouldn't win him any friends. You have to develop a faith that is disciplined enough to trust your reverence for God over your want of evidence.

You don't nurture a hungry faith on evidence; instead,

feed a hungry faith on reverence.

How to live with a faith that is hungry.

Develop a faith that questions. Discipline a faith that trusts reverence more then evidence. Demand that your faith not be scared of what God wants you to do. That's the real issue for most of us. We love God, we trust Him, and we believe that He is real, but if we are honest, we are scared of what it means to build an ark and to survive a flood and to stand on the other side with God looking to us to create a new world. What a burden. Or is it a blessing? We need to get past being afraid of what He might tell us to do. We can't be afraid to ask the question because we don't want to hear the answer.

Many of us won't take the step. We won't make the move. We won't give it a shot, and we won't start walking in that direction because we are scared. Looking at this metaphorically, I could say we are scared of what Pharaoh may say or what Ahab and Jezebel might do. We are scared of how strong Goliath may be, and we are afraid of seeing the giants. We are nervous about life outside of Egypt, and we are nervous about leaving the Ur of the Chaldees, wondering if we can ever go back to fishing again. But if you are going to live by faith, you have to defeat the fear you have of what God wants to do with and through you.

When I was called to preach, I postponed a position for the first twelve months of my career – not because I was scared of failing, but because I was scared of God succeeding. I knew if He succeeded in making me a preacher, it would mean a lifetime of presence in front of people, saying and shaping people to live for God, and that scared me. To this day, I fight to nurture a faith that is not afraid of how God uses me. And yet, when He does, I stand ready to receive what He wants me to do – no longer afraid.

Don't be afraid of what God is showing you. Don't be afraid of how God wants to use you. Don't be afraid of what He is telling you to give up or to take hold of. Don't fear what God is going to flow through you. He will make it work. He will make it happen. He will make it strong and powerful. And He will never give you a spirit of fear, instead, one of power, love and sound mind.

Don't be afraid; be steadfast, unmovable, and you will abound in the work of the Lord:

- You know your labor is not in vain in Him.

- He will accomplish what He shows you.

- He will bring it to pass, and you will overcome the enemy trying to stop you.

- Don't be afraid and don't be discouraged.

- God will only show you because He wants to be God through you!!!

Chapter 8: *Faith That Thinks*

*How far would you go to please God? How much
do you think you could give to a cause? To your
children? To your community – your environment?
How much sacrifice is too big? What should we
reasonably expect from ourselves? And when is
it time to think? Many times, we are faced with
violating God's will to save a fellow man. Many times
we nod in silent agreement when someone is punished
for a crime. Often, we profess to harm anyone who
would come near any of our family members with
malicious intent. Could we do something unthinkable
to please another – to please our God? Should we
think before we leap? It is not uncommon for fear or
ignorance to cloud what we think is right.*

A Father and Son

In the story of Abraham, we read with heavy hearts as Abraham looks at Isaac, his son, who is somewhere between 17 and 21 years old, and tries to hide from this beloved son that his heart is broken and that tomorrow will be the last day Isaac will breath God's precious air. You see, Abraham has been instructed by God in Genesis 22, to take his son to a mountain, which God intends to show him, and there offer him as a burnt offering before the Lord. We know that Abraham immediately responds in obedience and, the next morning, takes his son and two servants to follow God's will and sacrifice his son by his own hand at the mountain.

When Abraham arrives at the base of Mount Moriah, he discovers that he has reached the place where God expects his obedience to be carried to completion. Abraham doesn't waver; he responds immediately and binds Isaac, lays him upon the altar and takes the knife, preparing to thrust it through his heart when God stops him and shows him something unusual. A ram is alone on the mountain, caught in the thickets, so Abraham substitutes the ram for his son, and Isaac is spared. The fact that Isaac is spared is, obviously, important to Abraham because he carries a promise God made to him. Through Isaac, Abraham would father MANY nations, and he believes God to keep His promises. Abraham is also secure in the fact that he carried out his sacrifice obediently by choosing the ram. His servitude to God is apparent.

In Hebrews chapter 11:8-12, the writer interprets Abraham's mindset when getting ready to render his son as a burnt offering to God. We are given the reason Abraham was so calm about offering Isaac, and so resolute about following God in obedience. Many have, over the years, speculated that Abraham had no problem offering up Isaac because he was immersed in a culture that practiced child sacrifice anyway, and killing one's child was something that Abraham had grown accustomed to seeing while among strange cultures. Therefore, when he is asked to sacrifice

Isaac, though he does struggle with his emotional attachment to his son, he, nonetheless, has no problem with it in terms of societal implications because he was accustomed to seeing this practice. Many believe this.

Some suggest that Abraham is so afraid of the wrath of God that he would rather lose his son than attempt to disobey God and keep his son alive. In disobeying God, he felt the lives of he and his son would be worse – compromised or punished in some horrible way. But the writer of Hebrews gives us another consideration. The writer says that Abraham was at peace with the task of taking Isaac's life because he believed that God could raise him from the dead. By faith, Abraham, at the time of testing, offered Isaac back to God. Acting in faith, he was as ready to return the promised son, his only son, as he had been to receive him. Since Abraham knew that God had promised him Isaac, he figured that if God wanted to, he could raise the dead. In a sense, this is what happened when he received Isaac alive from off the altar.

Thinking about your obedience.

This line of thought introduces a faith that thinks; a faith informed by a sound and centered theology. Abraham was not robotically following God without applying his reasoning and processing to his faith. He believed in God and he knew he needed to do what God was telling him to do, but he also thought more deeply about what he was being asked to do. He didn't want to give up his son, and he certainly didn't want to slay his son. At the same time, he wanted to live obedient to God. After thinking a while about what he wanted, what he feared and who he loved, he was able to process the requests and he then clearly knew what God wanted him to do. He couldn't suggest that it would be okay to disobey God because God has been too good to him for him to ignore God's request. Weighing all of this, Abraham decides that he will have to go through with it and kill his beloved son if necessary. He also knows that God would not give him this promise, the promise of descendents from this only son, and then not fulfill the promise – in effect, kill it with Isaac, so he keeps thinking – reasoning – working through his faith.

Could God want me to hide my son until he is old enough? Can I hide from God? He knew he was talking about God, and his God had ultimate power. He could do what he wanted to do, and if he wanted to, he could raise this boy from the dead. After all, Abraham would be obedient; he would show true faith and devotion. And because he believes this, he follows through with an aggressive intent to kill his son. However, we know that God stops him.

Abraham's display of faith here is admirable; it is not a reckless faith, devoid of thinking and processing. He literally thinks his way through regarding how to be obedient to God and how to save his son at the same time – exhibiting love, strength and intelligence.

Abraham's thinking was so spiritual yet so cerebral and so focused on the character and strength of his God. He knew God had all power, and that God could choose to use some of that power to keep Isaac alive. All too often we find ourselves making tragic decisions that costs us precious time and energy and emotion because we don't exercise a faith that thinks. We react, we respond and this text teaches us that we must think. This is the kind of faith we are expected to develop.

Your faith can address the areas of confusion in your life. And we all have them. What to do with our lives? Why do other people seem to follow a strange or destructive path? We can't make sense out of what is going on in our world all of the time; life is too complicated and multi-dimensional. If you try to solely reason your way to enlightenment, you will be confused. And, if you try to solely pray your way to clarity, you will be confused. You need to have faith, and you need to think.

Abraham, without faith, wrestles with one central question that had to be gnawing at him and that is, why would God give him this promise (of descendents from Isaac) and then snatch it from him! God tells him that he will be the father of many nations through Isaac. He allows Abraham to father Isaac and begins to fulfill the promise, allowing Isaac and Abraham to live and prosper – that is, until Isaac grows to adulthood and then God tells him to kill Isaac, which will, in effect, kill the promise. How confusing. What was God trying to say? What was He trying to do? Was he trying to mentally challenge or break Abraham? Test him? Abraham never gives into his frustrations, however. He asks questions, and he exercises his theology. He exhibits true faith by seeking understanding, and he seeks until he finds something that makes sense. Isn't faith about asking questions?

We have to ask that question every time it appears that God is moving on our behalf and then, just as quickly, changes the course of his blessing. He opens a door and then, just as quickly, He shuts it.

Recently, I was delayed on a flight, coming home from a trip. When I got to my connecting city, my original connecting flight had already departed. Obviously, on the last leg of my trip, trying to get home, tired, hungry – just irritated, I was angry. No matter how I expressed how badly I wanted to get home, the attendant at the gate told me that my chances to get out of the city in a timely manner were not good. I got on a list to be put on the next available flight, and after a lot of blood, sweat, and tears, they found me a seat. I got on, put my bag in an overhead compartment, sat down in the seat, fastened my seat belt, closed my eyes and bowed my head to pray, as I always do before an airplane trip. As I was starting my prayers to thank God for getting me on the flight, keeping the plane safe in the air, protecting me while I am on the flight, helping us land safely, and even giving me strength to defeat anybody on this plane who decides to start acting disruptive, the flight attendant approached me. She informed me that I would be a weight violation for the flight, and that I would have to deplane and wait for the next flight home. I grabbed my bag, confused, and went and sat down in the concourse, waiting for the next flight. I sat there asking – God, why would you open a door and let me walk through it and then shut that same door? I still don't know why! Maybe something was going to happen, and He was sparing me. Maybe He was testing my fortitude or my ability to stay kind and accommodating in the face of frustration. Maybe He wanted to teach me a lesson about myself – to understand something inside of me that I hadn't acknowledged previously. Maybe He wanted me to take the experience to someone else and teach them tolerance and patience. It's hard to know why.

And this has to be where Abraham is, and his statement that he thought God could raise the boy from the dead was his answer to the confusion in his life – this awful dilemma with which he wrestled. He was confused about why God would ask this of him. Why would God renege on His promise? Why He would take so much away? Then, his faith reminded him that our earthly limits are not God's limits.

When you're so stressed that you can't breath, you find it difficult to move forward and stay positive. Try to remember that your limits are not God's limits. When you are at the point where you can't be stretched or tested any further, remember that God is not stressed or over-extended at all. And when you find yourself confused, rest on your faith in God and your faith in God will answer the confusing questions that life brings you. Why would God want Isaac sacrificed when God's promises were intended to flow through Isaac? Abraham's answer to all this was: God is able. Once Abraham rested there, he could then move to the next place, which is obedience.

The story of Abraham is an interesting progression. Obedience for Abraham can't be easy, especially when it comes to killing his son. However, Abraham appears to be at peace with it because his obedience is fed by his faith, and his faith is fed by the discovery that asking all those difficult questions about God's will provided him with the strength he needed. Many of us struggle with obeying God because we never seem to reach the right conclusions to our confusing questions, and this can be trying. Would we, in our current state of questioning, ever be able to answer why God would want to take away our only son, after giving him to us, or why God would let us go through such a horrible experience – a son dying at our own hands? And when you have no answer to the confusing questions in your life, you cannot make the decision that places you in the center of God's will. Abraham's faith in God addressed his confusion. We need to reach that same place in our own seeking.

Try to remember that your limits are not God's limits. When you are at the point where you can't be stretched or tested any further, remember that God is not stressed or over-extended at all.

An Enlightened Faith

I think we've established that his faith is not an ignorant faith; it is one born of thinking. When Abraham took these steps toward further enlightenment, he did so empowered with knowledge! His thinking led to the revelation that God could raise Isaac from the dead. This is interesting because it challenges us to wrestle with what kind of faith we have. I am convinced that many of us don't make the right decisions in certain areas of our lives because we refuse to think in relation to who we are in Christ. As Christians, we must process or consider what God asks of us – what we ask of ourselves daily – in tolerance, guidance, and servitude.

How did Abraham prepare for such a difficult task? Do you get the sense that Abraham processed this by devising various possible outcomes?

Maybe on the way, God will change his mind,

Maybe He will accept one of the servants in his place

Maybe He will let me be the substitute

Maybe He will shut the whole thing down.

God does none of these, He makes Abraham and Isaac walk the entire journey and Abraham at some point has to start thinking – no matter what happens, I believe that if I kill my son God has the power to raise him back up again. Do we trust God with such monumental decisions in our own lives? Do we trust our faith? Do we practice an enlightened faith?

God expects certain behaviors. He does. He just expects them from within the realm of what you can offer. He may test you – challenge you – but you can take that challenge, and… when it's time to think, He trusts you to reason it out – to use your faith. Abraham's faith was informed. He knew God well enough to know that God could raise Isaac from the dead. What's the depth of your relationship with God? Once you determine this, then you will be able to see what the potential of your life could be.

When popular syndicated radio hosts are offering spiritual advice, when entertainers are doubling as boot leg preachers, blending the mix of this contemporary spiritual pluralism, energized by secular humanism and guided by what professor, William Horton calls "moralistic therapeutic deism" it creates a situation in which we need a thinking clergy to preach to a thinking pew to wrestle with the real issue of life. And it has to be based upon the belief that there is only one God, manifested in three distinct characteristics: The Father, who created all; the Son who saves humanity; and the Holy Spirit who sustains our life as Christians. We need to believe that He created everything out of nothing. We need to believe that He sent His Son to such an unfathomable fate so that we might be free to worship Him in spirit and truth.

What is "the truth"?

Faith welcomes tests. I wonder when God first comes to
Abraham, even though the text doesn't say it, if he even
considered just not responding to God. After all, we certainly
would have understood such thinking if we were in the same
situation. I wonder if he contemplated just being disobedient. He
knew he was being stretched, challenged, and tested. And yet he
gets up the next morning and starts walking towards the agenda
God has mapped out for him.

Its almost like Abraham is energized by the challenge. He wants
to know God at a deeper level and be used at a deeper level, and
he welcomes whatever the path and plan to do that. Would we all
be able to do this? Ask yourselves. Do you really want to be the
best that God wants you to be? Can you embrace that true faith
will only come as you learn to get excited about the tests God
will send your way?

He loves you so much that He doesn't want to see you
stay where you are! He knows that there is more in you
– something greater in you, stronger in you, and He will
test you to get you to realize that, and you have to learn
to accept that and, in fact, to want that.

It is a hard pill to swallow sometimes. Consider this: He loves
you so much that He doesn't want to see you stay where you are!
He knows that there is more in you – something greater in you,
stronger in you, and He will test you to get you to realize that,
and you have to learn to accept that and, in fact, to want that.

What's the limit of your faith? You really don't know unless you
have been stretched and tested. How determined are you to stay
in God's will? You will only find this out when you are being
tempted and you are presented with a choice to do something

other than what God wants you to do. How far can God push you? You will only find the answer to that when you are pushed to your highest potential.

Abraham's said: "I believe in God not just until life ends: I believe God even in death that if He chooses to He can raise your Isaac from the dead".

What's your "give up point"? Do you believe that there is something that can separate you from the love of God? I don't! Believe that you are capable. God does too.

Remember, here is the truth:

- Nothing is too hard for Him.

- He is too much in love with us to leave us.

- He is able to do what we can't imagine.

- No human or angel or false God can minimize Him.

- He will never stop loving us.

- He will never stop wanting us.

Section 3

Applying Faith to Daily Life

Chapter 9: *A Faith To Be Corrected*

How many of us have watched as numbers, statistics, or people obsessed with worldly and trivial pursuits controlled our destiny? Have you ever encountered a basketball coach who relied entirely on his or her player's height, weight or scoring ability as opposed to the heart that some players may have – or the support some teammates may provide for the greater good of the game? Have you ever listened as the success of an event or party was based on the number of people in attendance as opposed to the fun had by all or the joy it brought everyone? I'm sure we've all even participated in such faithless pursuits, relying on numbers, who looks better or who is going to help us statistically or monetarily – as opposed to who is there for us in love – in faith. It's not hard to overcome this – it's not hard to change your focus.

King David

This chapter describes one of the lowest moments in King David's adventurous life. To provide some relevant background, David was the youngest of Jesse's sons and was almost overlooked for greatness his whole life, and yet, he achieved greatness. He succeeded, despite human attempts to keep him from this greatness or to make him believe that he wasn't capable of such accomplishments such as becoming a great warrior and a great king. David's rise to power was really anything but miraculous. His life had been marked by battle after battle, and David prevailed over the years, because in spite of all of his contradictions, David kept a heart for God. So, there were no miracles for David; he achieved every bit of what he garnered in life.

As king, he was finally able to enjoy the fruits of his labor and the rewards of having been a worshipper, yet David does experience a low – at a time just before he turns the kingdom over to his son, Solomon, who will fulfill his father's dream of building God a temple for his permanent holy dwelling place. The story of King David can be a haunting one, especially for those of us who are trying to live with a heart towards God, because, at the peak of his reign, David has a moment of true demonic vulnerability.

There is no indication regarding exactly what led him into this type of temptation. He wasn't fraught with bad news. He wasn't entertaining secret thoughts or participating in some secret activity that left him with a soiled spirit or invasive and evil thoughts. He has maintained his relationship with God, and he has not failed to keep up with his worship of God. And yet, David is harboring something in his heart that makes him vulnerable to Satan in this season unlike some seasons before. And it's interesting that Satan has always been trying, and God has been shielding David from this kind of influence. This time, however, David must be entertaining these thoughts – this action – in such a way that God removes the grace of protection from

David so that he is alone in entertaining and trying to resist the thoughts that are in his mind.

In I Chronicles 21:2-4, David says to Joab, I want you to count the people; I need to know how many fighting men we really have. Joab senses that David is going through something, and so he argues, saying – King, you don't want to do this; we have never had to do this in order to fight and win our battles.
He continues, saying – Our battles have never been about how big or strong our army is, but how big and strong our God is. However, David says he demands that the men be counted, and for nine months and some twenty days, they comb Israel and count hundreds of thousands of men who are enlisted specifically to fight or who can hold their own in a battle should they be needed. They bring this number back to God. Suddenly, David realizes the severity of what he has done. He has never won a battle simply because he has outnumbered his adversaries. He has never won a battle because his weapons were stronger than the weapons of his enemies. He has never won a battle because his military strategy was extremely sophisticated. In reviewing all of this in his mind, David realizes that he has committed his greatest sin in relying more on the strength of his men as opposed to the strength of his God, which he had always done in the past.

When you lose sight of who is really on your side.

David won his battles because God was on his side, fighting against his enemies, confusing his enemies, intimidating his enemies – yet, David, for nine months and twenty days, lives in a season where he is trusting what he sees more than who he knows. He is, in fact, trying to find security in what he can count rather than in the God who has protected him. Of course, history tells us that this dates back to a time in which, as a shepherd boy, he stood as the underdog in a fight against a giant and prevailed.

It is important to note here that God has not given David victory because of numbers of fighting men. God gave David victories throughout his life because God fights for worshippers – and… God knew David was faithful. What do you think spurred this low season in David's life and in his worship of God? I mean, we all have them, don't we? Low seasons, times of self-doubt, or loss of faith in our lives. Have you ever asked yourself "why am I doing this?" or what have I done?" – Surprised at your own behavior, as a Christian – as a contributing member of society? Do you think King David felt this way? I'm sure he did. In fact, we, as informed Christians, know he did. Be encouraged that you are no different than King David or anyone else. We all have times where we trust what we can see more than who we know. At times, we see the evidence of emptiness in our lives, and we make certain decisions to satisfy our own needs and further our own agendas instead of trusting a God who says, in very basic terms, "I've got your back". Don't turn your back on God. Don't bend the rules to make new friends – friends who will further an agenda that can otherwise be satisfied with one focus – faith in God and worship of Him.

Don't turn your back on God.

Don't bend the rules to make new friends

It became apparent to King David that he had sinned when he started hearing the numbers – the numbers of nameless, faceless people who could, supposedly, help him more than God could. And, he thought, "I have sinned. I have trusted the numbers to be my security against the attacks of my enemies rather than to trust the God who led me in battles when I was the underdog." And King David immediately confesses his sin, and, immediately, his spiritual advisor comes to him with a prophetic message from the Lord. He tells him, simply, "God is going to deal with your sin". Of course, David knows that, and don't we all know when we've sinned in such a way? In David's case, he is presented three options: Three years of famine in the land, three months of hard pursuit of your life from your enemies, or three days of plague in

the land. David actually doesn't hesitate. David knows he needs
to be corrected by God because his lack of faith warrants such
action. He says that he would rather fall into the hands of God
than into the hands of men, regarding correcting his life and
dealing with his mistakes. Isn't this where we'd all rather be – in
the Lord's hand when we are trying to get ourselves together? It's
a better place to be than in the hands of your fellow man, who is
also prone to error and vulnerable to sin. Wouldn't we all rather
deal with what God sends to correct us, than what our fellow
corruptible man would send to correct us?

Correction and our faith.

David's faith in God moves him quickly to a place where he trusts
God for his correction. He knows he has to be corrected, and he
only trusts God to do it. We all have to get to a place where our
faith is mature enough that its not just about having trust in God
to receive such blessings in life as miracles, answered prayers,
assurances, and promises. All these things notwithstanding,
we have to get to a place where our trust in God places our sins,
deviant thoughts, and contrary actions in His hands because we
trust God to deal with what we, obviously, aren't always capable
of handling. Life is tough, and He knows that. Trust Him to help
us – to correct our path – our faith – when we need it.

Do you trust God to give you what you need in terms of provision
and protection? Of course you do. He is such a loving God that
any blessing He gives is bigger than what we could create for
ourselves. But can we get to a place where we trust God to correct
us without any fear of how He will accomplish it, and with no fear
or reservation regarding what He might do to help us correct our
path? We can sin, but… we can't accept our correction. Maybe we
see it as punishment. Maybe we need to revisit our faith.

Trusting our conscience and what we know is right.

How do we know when God is stimulating our faith because
we need to be corrected? You know it when your conscience is

divinely invaded. What do I mean by this exactly? Well, this is what happens to David, isn't it? David becomes conscience-stricken, knowing that he has done something terribly wrong. Where was his conscience nine months and twenty days earlier? Why does David realize, almost ten months later, what he has done? In fact, where is our conscience when we know we've done something wrong in our own lives? I don't know the answer to that, but I do know that's where most of us live. We all know that feeling, don't we?

Well, here's what your faith does for you: It provides a back up to that side of you – that side that lets disobedient and "quick fix" solutions into your otherwise faithful path. Your worship of God – your trust in Him – is what provides the warning that tells you to back up – to move back into that place of true Christian pilgrimage. Who do you trust? Who has always been there for you? We all drive cars, and we all know that our car – that faithful vehicle that gets us where we need to go – will make a warning noise – a high-pitched beep that let's us know we are about to make a big mistake. It stops us before we crash backwards into something that is going to cause us harm – stop us in our tracks. That's what your faith does. When you are about to back into something that will move you from your path, your trust in God, which is born out of your relationship to Him, something starts warning you – beeping in your ear. You know you've heard it. Just make sure you listen.

You're too good for a life without faith.

David becomes conscience stricken and he confesses his sin, and God tells David's spiritual advisor to make a decision and David chooses quickly and wisely, saying I would rather fall into the hands of God than the hands of man. Why? Because a faith that corrects teaches us that God is always shaping our lives productively. In this case, David trusts that his God will show him mercy.

When I was a kid, my sister and I would get into a lot of trouble, as kids always do. My mother would, of course, be angry. We were a little intimidated by her wrath, but we knew her merciful side was much stronger than the side that wanted to punish us. My father, on the other hand, was a different story. His wrath was real. His need to punish far outweighed his need to show mercy. He would tell us what we had done wrong and make us reflect on it. To him – the lesson was more important than showing alliance to us. That was his way. However, my mother was different. In fact, when my mother got home, we would always meet her at the car and confess our transgressions because we trusted her to show us mercy and, now, in hindsight, I know we wanted to hear her correction for us – her legacy in understanding that shaped the way we grew. That was her way. And – that is God's way. David knew that. We know that. We are too good not to trust in our faith – in our relationship with God.

A faith that corrects teaches us that God is always shaping our lives productively.

How can we live with a faith that knows it needs to be corrected:

- Open your mind to others. Show love and show understanding.

- Open your heart to God. Live in His image – trust in His love.

- Never forget your faith; always revisit your relationship with God.

- Ask yourself if your path is true. You are better than your worldly pursuits. You do understand your life as a Christian. You know when you've done wrong.

- Trust God to correct your path. Know that getting back on track is most important.

- Be an example to your fellow man.

Chapter 10: *Faith To Accept Change*

I think we all reminisce about the good old days.
Those days might be high school. They might be
when our kids were little. They might be a time
with friends before we were married. Yet, despite
fond memories and current happiness, there is often
a longing to be that person again for just one day.
Then, we feel a bit of sadness, or we begin to reflect
on how hard it was to move through the stages of
our lives – to accept change, for better or for worse,
and to move on and become the people we need to be.
Change is hard sometimes, but a strong faith can see
you through it all.

The Story of Rahab

Rahab is a harlot and, while working her trade, she hears from her clients and conquests about the spiritual connection the Israelites are experiencing with a God called Jehovah who was helping them fight battles, defeat enemies, and claim land. Rahab hears this, and she hears about how this Jehovah, who is leading them, is taking them to the land of promise, a land called Canaan.

And Rahab processes what she hears, she listens with an open heart and mind, probably unconsciously looking for a change in her life, and she lets it plant a seed – a seed of faith. In fact, she begins to believe that this mysterious God of the Israelites is the true God, and that He will give to them exactly what is rumored – The Promised Land. As a result, Rahab leaves her life as a harlot, fully expecting that life will provide her an opportunity to attach herself to Jehovah. It doesn't matter that she is immersed in a pagan culture, among pagan practicing people; she grows faith and accepts that what she has been a part of and what her life has produced to date, is about to go through a change. Her comfort zone is about to be shaken up by God. She accepts this change, which had to be really hard, because nobody likes change.

Joshua had commissioned two brothers[1] from among the Israelites to go specifically into Jericho as spies in the hopes of ascertaining what might be the best method to use to defeat the city. These two men, no doubt, decide that probably the easiest place to hide out in the city, since they are strangers, is to hide out in the home of a harlot. It would not be unusual for strangers, visiting a new city where they know no one, to go into a house like that. Of course, that kind of house would not be conspicuous to anyone living a reputable life; no one would admit going there as citizens of the city.

Little do they know that Rahab, who lives in the house and used to live that kind of life, has developed an active faith life based upon what she and her people have heard about God. This

God, they hear, is said to be advancing the Israelites towards occupation of The Promised Land. Despite the fact that she has not walked the path the Israelites have walked or seen the miracles that God has performed for them and with them, Rahab, nonetheless, has allowed what she hears to so impact her life that she develops confidence in this God. It affects how she receives these spies, and it guides what she asks in return of them. In Hebrews[2], we understand that she receives them and hides them by faith. Rahab, a former harlot, gives safe haven to two spies and, beyond that, allows them to take privileged information back to the Israelites regarding how to defeat Jericho. She knows it must be done; Jericho is not a good place. She knows this through her faith.

Most remarkably is that Rahab hides these two brothers in her upper chamber, which is very risky, and when word arrives that two strangers are in town and have been seen going into her house, a small delegation goes to her house and inquires about the two strangers. She tells the delegation nothing, and, beyond that, when they are gone, she safely lowers the strangers to the ground and simply asks that she and her family be spared when God's wrath levels Jericho. She does this – and asks this – for and of two strangers! By faith.

Accepting a Wave of Change

Leonard Sweet in his book <u>Soul Tsunami</u> talks about life as a series of waves, and when the wave of change comes, you have but two options. One is to prepare for it, and when it comes, jump the surfboard and ride the wave to shore, which means to expect the change and go with it. Another way is to watch the wave come in and remain determined not to do anything, thereby getting washed under by it. Of course, the point is to accept change when it comes your way.

There are some of us who, in Rahab's place, would not have accepted change, and, therefore, would not have hid the spies and would not have been spared God's wrath. In fact, can you honestly say that you would have accepted change, defied your current way of life and let faith guide your rehabilitation? Most of us would be more comfortable with the familiar and the usual and, then, unfortunately, we would have been destroyed as change wiped out our sin-ridden city. Some of us would fight change and become defenders of the status quo until absolute destruction would have proven us wrong.

Change is a part of faith.

Strong faith becomes comfortable with constant change. Even in our churches, we are experiencing change. We preach a changeless Gospel but to a changing world. We don't listen to sermons now like people did in 1980, where poetry and long sermonic tension were appealing to people. Today, people want to say directly to the preacher – so how does this apply to me? Life is more immediate, and churches and preachers have to adapt to that need. It is simply change. The Gospel still speaks to us as fresh as it did to those Jesus introduced it to many years ago. Church isn't always defined by who comes into the building anymore; people watch and listen to me on the Internet, and I would have never imagined that. I can affect people I've never even met. In fact, there are members of my church who are "cyber members" and who are more faithful and more giving than some who physically come to the building. This is a change for me – one that I had to accept. I feel that to not want change is to resist the invitation of faith to grow to the next level in your relationship with God.

I know some of us still want a cassette tape in an iPod season; we want a big luxury gas-guzzling car when hybrids are the way of the future. We still think Shaft is the latest in style, and we are upset when, instead of Shaft, we get Jay Z in P. Diddy's Sean Johns. Change is taking place, and faith will require that you change as well. After all, does any of this change seem bad? Maybe an iPod is a little high tech at first, but you get used to it.

And, face it, Jay Z is just as cool and stylish as Shaft; it's just in a different way.

People used to get hired at a company and stay there for 30 years. They would retire and enjoy life. Now, the average person will go through approximately six job changes in a lifetime. That's a lot of change! And faith is the only internal guarantee that we have that helps us through a life of constant change. We are who we are – no matter what – through good and bad – because of faith.

Faith is the only internal guarantee that we have that helps us through a life of constant change. We are who we are, no matter what – through good and bad – because of faith.

Examine your loyalties.

You need faith to accept change because all change calls for an examination of ones loyalties. Rahab is an example of this. She was immersed in:

- Pagan culture
- Harlot lifestyle
- A city about to be taken over by Nomads

She Hears about Jehovah and knows the following to be true:

- The way He is leading the Israelites
- The promises He has made
- The battles He has helped them win

She is immersed in a lifestyle that is opposite what she is hearing; however, she changes and plants her loyalties with Jehovah. This is demonstrated in how she embraces the spies and what she says to them. Joshua 2:9-11:

I know that the Lord has given you the land – that the terror of you has fallen on us, and that all the inhabitants of the land are fainthearted because of you. For we have heard how the Lord dried up the water of the Red Sea for you when you came out of Egypt, and what you did to the two kings of the Amorites who were on the other side of the Jordan, Sihon and Og, who you utterly destroyed. And as soon as we heard these things, our hearts melted. Neither did there remain any more courage in anyone because of you, (and here is where her loyalties switched) "for the Lord your God, He is God in Heaven above and on earth below".

From harlot to faith in Jehovah – and from pagan worshipper to faith in Jehovah. Look at the difference in her loyalties. What she has become in God, a faithful believer, from what she used to be, a common harlot, is a remarkable and strong faith statement. Are you capable? Ask yourself.

No matter what else faith is, it will make you examine your loyalties and whatever stands between you and complete trust and faithfulness to God will always be held in tension. Have you noticed that? That the more you attempt to grow in faith, the more tension you have in many areas and it's because faith calls for examination of loyalty. You feel this pull – this uncomfortable place because this is not an easy thing to do – to honestly look within – at where you really place your faith.

I have heard many people talk about their desire to get out of debt. They feel the pain of debt – they are unable to contribute to the church, their community, and they want financial freedom. They are, however, tied to their financial habits like Rahab was tied to the ways of Jericho. They still want to spend money all the time – they won't employ a strategy to work towards financial freedom – and they still won't give a tithe or an offering to God. We know these people. And while the confession of faith is that they want financial freedom and life without debt, the loyalties have not changed. And faith demands that they do. They will have to see money differently – prioritize and see debt as distraction and tithe for God an investment with high return – and, above all, that they need to discipline themselves or deny themselves from time to time to live differently – and better. This is a hard thing to do.

Embrace Transition

Faith to accept change is to also embracing transition. Rahab is used to having men in her house, but not men like this. She has to make a transition based on faith – from men who only want her for her services, to men who believe her faith in their God is honest and true. She begins to understand that relationships are not just for taking but for giving as well. This God that she has come to trust and believe bestows so much on the faithful, so she can give two men in need a place of hiding with no price attached. She allows herself a transition for how she deals with these strangers and with the men in her city of Jericho who are looking for these Israelites. She sends her fellow city-dwellers on a wild goose chase –a big change for her, but a symbolic bridge that she uses to transition from harlot of Jericho to faithful follower of God.

Faith calls for constant transition. Faith helps you over the bridge of change. Many of us have a difficult time facing the fact that we need transitions to allow the change to work completely and honestly in our lives. These are big, scary differences – having to live by a different routine – having to do something different, different than what we have been doing all our lives. A different life is going to call for a different method, a different lifestyle, a different approach, and more. This is not comfortable. It is not unreasonable to allow ourselves a transition. God allows it; accept it and move on.

Life is constant change.

Living single for so long, I learned to enjoy my life – to come and go as I pleased. My habits never had competition. What I did with my space didn't need any other opinion. To get married and to have to consider another person's feelings or to embrace another person's wants was very new to me. A lot of us have been there. It is exceedingly difficult to be challenged by another person's differences in habits and expectations. The struggles that occur when we make someone a part of our lives often make us think that the other person doesn't love us. Of course, it's not always that he or she doesn't love you; it could be that he or she or you are having a hard time transitioning.

A different life is going to call for a different method, a different lifestyle, a different approach, and more. This is not comfortable. It is not unreasonable to allow ourselves a transition. God allows it; accept it and move on.

I remember the time I received a Sony PlayStation® for my birthday, and I set it up in the basement and got ready to play. Much to my dismay, I couldn't beat my grade school-aged daughter at one game consistently because she transitions to new ideas and mindsets quicker than I do, and I am still trying to figure out the last move when I need to be on the next one. I'm working on it, but... thus far, this transition is hard for me – but... not for her. That is sometimes difficult to accept too – that others may transition a little easier than you do. Be patient – have faith. It will happen.

The President of the United States, Barack Obama, is a clear example of how one person defied convention, facilitated change, accepted his responsibility as a leader, and became the huge success that he is today. President Obama had to follow his faith; he had to believe that accepting the challenge that God presented him was going to cause a change in his life for the better. He took that path, in faith and without fear, and became the first African-American president of the United States of America, overcoming political, racial and ideological opponents. Did he know that this was God's plan for him when he first felt the call to change this country – this world – for the better? Did he trust that, for all his hard work, for all the fortitude it required to stay this path and accept change – even lead that change – that it would result in becoming the leader of the free world and even being awarded the Nobel Peace Prize? One thing is certain, he must have known in his heart and in his mind that this change was right. He had that sense of faith; a faith to accept and even champion change, which we can all learn from and strive to pursue.

You have to become comfortable with transitions and transitions are comfortable when embraced in faith.

Faith to Accept Change

So, what gave the harlot, Rahab, the right to think that she deserved to be spared with the kind of life she had lived? How many people had she corrupted? How many houses had she destroyed? How many men developed a skewed view of love, sex and relationships because of her? And yet she asks to be spared. What gave her the right? Her faith! Her faith was strong. She was strong and unwavering, and she was open to accepting her change – her transition – and she embraced it.

In fact, Rahab had confidence that when you live to do what God tells you to do, you have a stake in God's plans. I have that kind of faith; I honestly believe that God keeps challenging us, God keeps chipping away at us, and God keeps pressing us all because He has plans to use us in the future. Your faith has to accept that and, further, celebrate that God will never let you go.

Faith helps you transition because faith gives you confidence that God is not taking you somewhere just to leave you there. It is a movement – a temporary place. You have to become comfortable with transitions and transitions are comfortable when embraced in faith.

Change is comfortable when embraced in faith. Consider this: Faith speaks to the fear of transitions and, therefore, speaks, too, to accepting change. So remember:

- If God is moving you, He is where you are moving. Don't be afraid.

- If He is making you leave something behind, He intends to replace it with something more necessary when you get where He is taking you, physically, spiritually, mentally. Don't mourn for something that isn't worth a second thought; instead, look to your future with Him.

- If He won't let what used to make you comfortable work anymore, He is intending on forcing you to change for the better, to transition – to accept a new faith, a new way. Don't shy away from it.

- If He is pulling different emotions and gifts and talents and skills out of you, it's because you will need them where He is taking you. Again, don't be afraid.

Endnotes

1 Joshua 4

2 Hebrews 11:31

Chapter 11: *Faith To Fit You*

What do you think you are meant for in this life? Were you called to a life in medicine? Were you called to a life of service to others? Maybe you're artistic or an athlete – or maybe you like to cook. We're all intended for something in this life, and we are all suited to those specific professions or interests. We have preferences and nuances to our personalities that guide us in our life's decisions. Do we live in the city? Maybe we prefer the suburbs. Some people like chocolate ice cream – others vanilla – and... still others don't like it at all. Faith is like that; it comes in all forms and suits all people. The key is finding your niche in this realm of faith.

The Power of Faith

Faith will operate powerfully in the life of any person who will dare to listen to God's word and surrender to God's will. It is why Paul was so confident to suggest that faith comes by hearing and, more specifically, hearing the word of God. The writer of Hebrews has given pointed attention to how important faith is in the life of a person by listing people who were able to do amazing things for the kingdom once they allowed their lives to be lived in faith.

In Hebrews 11:32, there is a list of people who are noted for how they operate in faith. This list represents quite a variety of personalities and quite a range in interpretations of faith. It follows:

- Gideon – a frightened farmer whose faith did not grow strong right away.

- Barak – who by faith won a great victory over Sisera, but his faith needed human support and God sent to him the prophetess, Deborah, to bring assurance to him that God was with him and that God would work through him.

- Samson – whose faith was the singular reason he made a comeback after a tragic mistake.

- Jephthah – whose faith made him live up to vows he made to the Lord because even when facing a tough decision that he didn't want to make, faith helped him choose conviction over convenience.

- David – who had faith that helped him face and fight giants.

- Samuel – whose faith helped him tell the truth even to people this truth would adversely affect.

And, so, let's examine what these flawed, ordinary people were able to do through faith:

- Subdue kingdoms
- Work righteousness
- Obtain promises
- Stop the mouths of Lions
- Quench the violence of fire
- Escape the edge of the sword
- Live strong with weaknesses
- Fight bravely in battle
- Make stronger armies flee
- Have stuff that died, given back to them alive
- Embrace suffering for a greater reward

Amazing, right? Or – are these simply accomplishments that can be tackled and won with a little bit of faith? Yes. In fact, the point here is that there is nothing you could want to become in life that faith can't create for you! Look at what faith did for these personalities listed in this text. All that they conquered, all that they became, what they accomplished, and what they attained is all due to faith. There is nothing you could want to become in life that faith in God can't create for you.

- Significance
- Impact
- Adventure
- Strength
- Success
- Influence
- The power to make a difference.

Again, there is nothing so unique in life that faith can't create for you. Do you want your footprint on this world to mean something? Do you want even just the time you spend with your family to be impactful? Do you want to be perceived as strong, adventurous, successful and influential, and... beyond that.... do you ask for the fortitude to have it all? Faith is what allows and fuels this need to make a difference. It is what gives you that necessary power to do so. And really, what can hold you in bondage so securely that faith can't overcome? What can threaten you so badly that you forget the security you have in Christ? Nothing. Faith does it all. There is nothing so unique that faith can't assist with, create or overcome. This is shown to us again and again in Hebrews **11** and by daily example in our everyday lives.

There is nothing you could want to become in life that faith in God can't create for you.

Faith fits everybody.

We witness in Hebrews 11 the diversity of the people known for their intense faith, the differences in their backgrounds, and the struggles they had to endure in order to live for God. And how did they do this? They did it by developing strong faith in God. And of course the lesson is that faith fits everybody – no matter your race, size, socio-economic status or profession. There is a faith to fit you.

We do see this in our daily lives. For example, some people are made for only certain types of clothing. One woman may wear a skirt that others would feel is too short. Some men will never wear a sweater and, instead, prefer dress shirts or polos. It is a simple preference and each article of clothing works – for certain people. Some people are suited for certain types of jobs. I could not be a surgeon, nor could I work in a place where everyday I had to deal with people who are physically abused. I have low tolerance for the bloody and too much want of revenge for the victim to work those jobs. I know what I am suited for – a life preaching God's Word. And while there are many who try to tell me how to do my job, I know that I am fit for that which God called me to do. This is what I do well. This is how I make my living. We are all a good fit for a life of faith, however. Faith is a personal and individual thing. We see that; we feel that. God wants us to be comfortable – to approach and worship Him the best way that we can – our own way.

Faith is never a "bad fit".

There is nothing about you that makes faith a bad fit for you. That's why we've examined so many here who functioned so powerfully in faith and in so many different ways. We have seen the following types of people:

- Weak
- Timid
- Scared
- Tough
- Stubborn
- Prone to mistakes
- Selfish
- Ambitious
- Hot-tempered

We have seen, too, that faith fit them all to the glory of God. And, guess what? Faith will fit you too. So, we have to pose certain difficult questions to ourselves.

First, what is our excuse for not living a life of faith? Many times, we say that it is our background. We have suffered so much or been exposed to so little in terms of faithful people that we can't muster up some faith ourselves. Often, we tell ourselves that life isn't fair; we are lacking something in our lives or our prayers have not been answered. Maybe we feel that past mistakes are keeping us from a life close to God. Are we simply afraid to put so much stock in faith? Maybe we even feel that there are better options for us out there.

Perfection is not what God wants.

And here is the truth that we must celebrate and affirm. God is so good that He strengthens us through faith, not perfection. None of these people, all with different personalities, were mentioned for their perfection; they were all listed and praised for their faith. Faith, in effect, erased their flaws as they were remembered in the Kingdom of God. God doesn't expect us to be perfect; he expects us to have faith in order to overcome obstacles and live a life of service to Him and to others.

God is so good that He strengthens us through faith,

not perfection.

Did any of these characters have a story without regret and missteps? Did any of them have immediate success and a life without any obstacles or challenges? No, not one of them. All of these people had a lifetime of obstacles and challenges and mistakes and regrets, and despite all that, they made it into the esteemed "hall of faith". If they overcame so much to live a faithful life, it is difficult, then, for any of us to live using the excuse that our lives are not sanitized enough or "straight and narrow" enough to live for God in faith. Faith changes the criteria for how life and, really, God evaluate you. Don't rely on the same old excuses – your fear, your past, your inability to trust your own gifts, your inability to take life seriously; none of these are valid. What is valid is that all these people before us lived by faith, and that erases all excuses.

The Upgrade

I remember years ago when I participated in a conference of pastors from across the country that met in the Bahamas, and I took my family with me. My ticket, because of how often I travel, was in first class, and my wife and daughter were in coach. I got on the plane, and after everybody settled in their seats, I went back and asked the gentleman who was sitting next to my wife would he mind taking my seat in first class so that I could sit back here with my wife. Now, I was offering him an opportunity to have larger seating, free beverages, a hot meal, less noise, free earphones for the movie, unlimited snacks and more, but I suppose he didn't think about how much he would be really getting, and he began with all these odd excuses such as: I don't know if they would still have overhead space for my belongings; I am already strapped in; we are close to take off; and on and on. For each excuse, I kept giving him answers that were intended to help him to see that he was being offered something so awesome for free that he ought to jump on it immediately. He couldn't see this, however, because he was settled into his excuses. Another man, on the other side of the aisle, adjacent said, "I will take you up on that offer if you want to be close to your family." As he got up to go sit in first class, he said to the man who had been so full of excuses, "You don't know what you just turned down on a long flight like this."

Don't rely on the same old excuses – your fear, your past, your inability to trust your own gifts, your inability to take life seriously; none of these are valid.

That's how we should feel as it relates to faith in our lives. It's an upgrade from having to fly through life by sight, and it brings some upgrade privileges, unlimited access to the pilot and unending resources to strengthen you for the journey of life. It comes with provision and protection; in fact, to not adopt a life of faith leaves the faithful, like me, absolutely incredulous. Just as the man who would not upgrade to first class was set in his ways, we can become set in our ways. But, why? Why would we deny ourselves such an upgrade?

Excuses

What are your excuses? Beyond that, for those who have battled your excuses, what is your delay? What could you possibly want to do or be or have that could keep you from living in faith? What better options are there? We have now examined how ordinary people with ordinary lives became extraordinary shining examples of faith just by believing and allowing themselves that upgrade – that movement to a better life.

With all that is so uncertain in our world, how can you delay your movement to faith? We live in a world desperate for the faithful to rise and lead. In this country alone, we hear news daily of shootings in malls and schools. We have to worry daily about terrorist attacks from other places and from within our own borders. We are suffering from an economy now that is broken by greedy credit card companies and a sub-prime mortgage industry that has broken many homeowners dreams. Unemployment is high, and natural disasters plague us every season in all parts of the world. Where can we find safety and security in this world? Nowhere, but in finding faith in Jesus Christ.

What could you possibly want to do or be or have that

could keep you from living in faith?

What do you have a taste for? A need for?

I was in Indianapolis recently, preaching to a congregation of people. While there, my host took me to a nice restaurant, but, of course, I had never been there before. We sat down, and the waitress asked me what I had a taste for, and I asked her, "Well, what do you recommend?" She asked me if I had ever tasted their salmon, which they prepared with special care each night.

She spoke cheerfully but with some conviction about where it was from, and that it was the finest. She went into depth about the marinade, the chef's precision in cooking it and more. I really don't remember exactly what she said, but I can tell you this; when she was done, I said with a lot of conviction (and with my mouth watering), "I'll have that!"

Where can we find safety and security in this world?

Nowhere, but in finding faith in Jesus Christ.

That's what God is asking you, really. What do you have a taste for in life? And if you need a recommendation, he will suggest that you order a healthy portion of faith. It is prepared hillside and slow prepared for three days and on the third day, when it is removed from the oven of sin and death, it is bread sent down from glory, that is guaranteed to fill your soul.

Try it. You will like it. Now, one last list; a list of what you will gain – what you will enjoy – if you listen to what God recommends and develop a taste for the finest He has to offer – faith. Here's what you'll miss if you don't try:

- Forgiveness
- Strength
- Victory
- Resurrection
- Deliverance
- Second chances
- Power
- Wisdom
- Assurance
- Protection

Chapter 12: *Faith To Make The Tough Decisions*

How often have we prayed to God to make an ailing loved one feel better? How many times have we prayed to ask for guidance in a difficult decision? How many times do we defer to God and not allow our own faith to provide the guidance we need? Do we always feel that we need assurance from others or a blessing before we make these vital or difficult decisions?

Joseph, his Father and his Sons

Word has reached Joseph that his father Jacob is fading fast;
it won't be long before he will go from time temporal to time
eternal. Joseph grabs his two sons, Manasseh and Ephraim, and
he quickly makes his way to his father's bedroom where, laying on
his deathbed is Jacob, a man whose life has been so shaped by the
hand of God that even his limp tells the story of how intentional
God has been in his life[1]. Joseph carries a certain urgency that is
apparent in his approach. This urgency is far beyond just being
present for these final hours of his sainted father's life.

He carries another agenda. He wants his father to bless his two
sons and to transfer a divine agenda to each of their respective
lives. When he arrives with his sons, Manasseh and Ephraim, he
positions them in front of his father, who with slanted eyes can
distinguish that his son, Joseph, is present, but he is unclear who
else is there. Slowly, he gathers enough strength to kick his legs
from beneath the covering on the bed and with strained effort, he
shifts until he is seated on the side of the bed. His eyes are dim
and his strength is fading, but the level of his connection to God
is still sharp, and he inquires about the two men who are present
in his private chamber with his son, not recognizing that they are
his own grandsons. Joseph tells him that these are his boys, and
Jacob says bring them to me so that I can bless them.

Joseph knows that the son he puts in front of his father's right
hand will receive the eldest sons blessing (more promise, more
potential, and more prosperity) and because Joseph knows
this, he positions the eldest son on Jacob's right hand side and
Ephraim on the left, with the real hope that Jacob would bless
them equally. And as if Jacob is being led by the divine streams
that are still flowing active and intense in his life, he feels led by
God to lay his right hand on young Ephraim and his left hand on
Manasseh, and he gives the boys his blessing:

"God before whom my father's Abraham and Isaac walked. The God who has fed me all my life long to this day. The angel who has redeemed me from all evil, bless the lads. Let **my** name be named upon them. And the name of my fathers Abraham and Isaac and let them grow into a multitude in the midst of the earth."[2]

Joseph sees Jacob's hands crossed on the heads of his boys, and he wants to make sure the oldest son receives the traditional blessing. He tried to remove Jacob's hands in an attempt to reverse the blessing order, and Joseph, in essence, says, "Father, you have this wrong; Ephraim is not the eldest." Jacob says, "I know son; I am not doing what you want me to do, and I can't do what they want me to do. I am doing what I feel God wants me to do. Manasseh will be great but Ephraim will be greater, and his descendents will become a multitude of nations."

Can you imagine the tension of this moment? Joseph, of all people, knows the danger of sibling tension when things are not governed by tradition. After all, his own upbringing with his brothers and the favoritism of his own father towards him created some tension in his own young life. Therefore, naturally, Joseph wants them to receive what is traditional – the eldest endowed with the greatest destiny and the youngest accepting the cultural norm as second to his older brother. Joseph feels that Jacob has upset that, and maybe, what Joseph fears is that his father is setting his sons up to be rivals one generation removed from his own pain and angst with sibling rivalry.

How tough does your faith make you?

How determined, how resolute and how unyielding is your faith? Is your faith tough enough to switch the hands of your dreams or the hands of your ambitions, or the hands of your desires and lay them on God's choice for you rather than your choice for you? Could you have the conviction of Jacob and the trust of Joseph? Could you accept the weight of what you had been given or what had been taken away like Manasseh and Ephraim?

Is your faith so rigid, so restricted, so narrow, and so self absorbed, so limited that to shift your concentrations and attention is a struggle for you, and you are more convinced that God needs just to be told that He has it wrong? Further – that YOU need to assist Him in getting it right?

Faith, when it calls for you to grow and to really be who God wants you to be, will demand, at times, that you give in to some tough decisions that appear out of order, out of the norm, and away from common practice.

I remember distinctly the pride my father felt being my supervisor at the company where he ran the computer operating department and where I was blessed to work part-time. Obviously, the plan was for me to go to college to study computers, and then work as a programmer and eventually take his position. That was his plan; it was the owner's plan and, at one point, it was my plan. I enrolled at Morgan State University and immediately declared a major in Computer Science. When God called me to ministry, He switched the hand of my attention and concentration. Basically, He did what Jacob did and laid His right hand on my spiritual convictions and ministry calling and laid His left hand on my computer interest. I was on my way to a life in ministry. I went and talked to my father, and I remember as if it were yesterday his initial fear and concern. And, like Joseph, he tried to convince me that God must have just crossed the signals and that He meant to lay His right hand on my computer future and His left hand on my ministry calling. But … I felt the presence of God so strong for ministry and told him that I was changing my major to religious studies and philosophy and leaving the company to go work at the church. This was the toughest decision I had ever made at that juncture in my young life. But … I did it. I made it. I trusted in God and His plan for me. My father eventually understood too. And, aren't we all always kneeling before God in terms of what we want God to bless and anoint? Don't we ask for His direction all the time? Why, then, would we second-guess His plan for us?

Our Struggle.

Many of us are kneeling before God in terms of our direction in life and our desire for God to touch that ultimate direction – that right path for us – with his right hand. Here is the struggle, however; we don't always agree with where God places His right hand, do we? He lays his right hand on where we're asking for help rather than on our desire for pleasure and enjoyment. Why is His right hand on our academics but not our finances? Why is He granting good grades and a direction in life instead of bestowing us with millions of dollars? Remember this: Faith has to be able to accept where God places greater value and attention and expectation.

Faith, when it calls for you to grow and to really be who God wants you to be, will demand, at times, that you give in to some tough decisions that appear out of order, out of the norm, and away from common practice.

The truth is, mature faith will put you in some tough spots. If you are Joseph in this text or Manasseh or Ephraim, then you have to accept the will of God when it clashes with what you expected or anticipated or desired. When faith puts you in those tough spots, you have to trust that God has a reason, that God has a reward for your faithfulness, and that God has resources for what He requires. Listen to what Jacob tells Joseph, "I know which order you wanted, and I know this upsets you, but I am going to bless them both and both will have lives and legacies of which you will be proud, and from which God will get glory. But... this has to be the order – whether you like it or not – the younger brother is going to do great things."[2] He basically says, I know you want Manasseh to have a more noble future than Ephraim, but God wants something different. If Ephraim doesn't get what God has for him, there will be huge repercussions to both he and Manasseh. If Ephraim gets what he should get, then Manasseh will have a great life too, but you (Joseph) must understand that the younger will have more impact on the kingdom than his older brother.

How did Jacob do it?

He is dim in vision, he carries the scar of Joseph's journey, he has his own regrets about his life and his journey, and yet he resists Joseph's attempts to change what he feels is the will of God for the two that kneel before him. He does what he feels; he trusts God. In fact, the text says that after he blesses the boys, he leans on his staff and worships God[3]. Worshipping God is understandable; after all, he had been doing that for years. You don't wrestle with God and not become a worshipper, but he does so leaning on his staff, which is significant to note here.

When faith puts you in those tough spots, you have to trust that God has a reason, that God has a reward for your faithfulness, and that God has resources for what He requires.

Some have suggested that what is really meant here is that Jacob doesn't lean on his own staff but leans on Joseph's staff, which has on it an image of Joseph disagreeing with him. Others have suggested that what he does is turn himself on his bed so his face is toward the pillow and he worships, but there is no indication of the presence of the staff in that suggestion. Still others have suggested that he grabs the headboard of his bed, and he leans against it for support and worships God.

It is clear from the text that when he steadies himself on his staff, he worships. Is the staff a reminder of the burden born of abandoning the wants of his son? Disappointing him? Does he look to God for guidance and the strength to oppose someone right in front of him and whose wishes are so important to him?

Interesting. **When we are in the midst of tough decisions, God is clearly the one on whom we need to lean.** No matter how tough it gets – no matter how much pressure you face or how many people are trying to persuade you to do something different, you HAVE to keep leaning on your relationship with God.

What reminds you that God is your source of strength?

I don't know what your symbol of faith is and I don't know what your sign of faith is. Maybe we should ask ourselves daily for reminders of how good God has been to us – shaping us, being patient with us. Is there maybe a scar, from a surgery or an accident, that you bear which reminds you of what God rescued you from or used as a vehicle to reveal Himself? Is it maybe your children, your possessions, your freedom, your marriage, your opportunities, your sane state of mind – all such precious things that remind you of what you have through God? And, whatever this symbol is, like Jacobs staff, does it stimulate worship in you? It should.

When we are in the midst of tough decisions, God is clearly the one on whom we need to lean. No matter how tough it gets, no matter how much pressure you face or how many people are trying to persuade you to do something different, you HAVE to keep leaning on your relationship with God.

I have a gash on the bridge on my nose right between my eyes. This scar reminds me of a couple things. First, it reminds me of a late summer night trying to rush home on my bicycle before my father's curfew. I was in such a hurry that I crossed an intersection at the same time a late model Chevy Impala was coming through that light at full speed. It clipped the end of my bicycle and sent me flying into the air in the direction of the side of a house on the corner. I can still see it. I blacked out and woke to blood gushing. I couldn't give those who had come to my rescue my name or my address, and I remember hearing one of them say, "Just call the police; we don't know what this boy has been up to." When I look in the mirror every morning to brush my teeth, to shave, to comb my hair, to clean the sleep out of my crusted eyes – to this day, as a grown man, I worship God because that scar, my staff, stimulates me and reminds me that everyday is a gift from God.

What is upsetting is the way our culture disregards the staffs that remind us of our history with God. We no longer recognize the symbols of our faith. In thinking we know best all the time – in focusing on what we think we need as opposed to what God is trying to tell us, we are changing the language of our faith. We are dismissing the pioneers of our faith, and we need to be reminded that Jacob leaned on his staff to worship, reflect and remember the blessings and the struggles in his life and with his people. This reflection led to an important revelation. We need to listen to our faithful past. Faith is really surrendering to the life God wants from you more than it is the ability to get God to accept the life you want.

A good life comes with a lot of responsibility. Our daily routine can take quite a toll on us mentally, physically and spiritually. The struggle for bread and shelter continues, to the very end, beating at our lives and our very spirits with an insistence that cannot be ignored. For many, there are additional cares that go beyond the demands of our own personal survival and encompass the tender threads of the lives of others to whom we are bound by ties of blood and birth. This is all a lot to manage. Beyond all that, there are dreams, hopes, and yearnings, which occupy our minds as well.

There comes a moment within all of us when we are in utter revolt – something deep within us becomes tired, weary, exhausted and, finally, outraged. What we long for in this deep anxiety is some haven, some place of retreat, some time of quiet where our bruised and shredded spirits may find healing and restoration. One form that this anxiety takes is to hate life and to fear tomorrow. However, if we make our lives offerings and dedications to God, then this faithfulness will include all of our entanglements and involvements – and all of our answers and deliverances. He will help us.

Faith is really surrendering to the life God wants from you more than it is the ability to get God to accept the life you want.

Consider this about God. Keep all this in mind the next time you want to second guess the message of faith He is trying to give you:

- He has been good to you.

- He has been walking with you even through the bitter experiences of your life.

- When you cried, He did dry your tears.

- When you were scared, He did calm you fears.

- And when you prayed, He took away the doubt.

- He has made your life what it is today. Trust Him.

Endnotes

1 Genesis 32:22-30

2 Genesis 48:16

3 Genesis 48:17-22

Section 4

The Challenges of Faith

Chapter 13: *Faith To Overcome Fear*

Fear comes in many forms. It is the single mother afraid she can't feed her kids and, so, will go to great lengths to make money any way she can, often never realizing her own potential or dreams. It is the father of three daughters, afraid to send any of them off to college for fear of losing them to career or marriage or friends. And, it is sometimes simply just the basic fear that your family will not stay safe, that someone will get sick, that something will happen to the house that you live in. It is all these things and more. Putting your faith in God can alleviate so much worry, relieve so much fear.

One of the obstacles of faith is fear.

Fear attempts to meet faith at the intersection of real spiritual courage and force doubt into the one pondering a faithful life. I have watched people miss more opportunities, not because those opportunities were so impossible or that they would require so much strength and might, but rather because the person was afraid of whether it could truly happen for them or whether they would be crushed permanently for thinking they could live life at these courageous levels.

Think for a moment about how much in your life has been held up, held back or held still because you didn't know how to answer fear when it required an explanation as to why you were attempting to move forward, or to take a chance, or to get better, or to demand more of your life. Fear is an enemy to faith. Peter, one of the Lord's disciples, had allowed faith to so motivate him that late one night out on choppy waters in a rough storm, he found himself walking on water – a reward of the faithful. However, Peter listened to fear tell him that he shouldn't be walking on water, despite the fact that Jesus was present, and when Peter surrendered to his fear, he began sinking – yet, a moment ago he was walking on the water that was now enveloping him. Hard to believe? No. It's no different for us. We can certainly understand that feeling. Many times, we are on a path and moving at a good pace, and then… we let fear take over our actions and lose momentum. The enemy to faith is fear, and the moment you allow fear into your spiritual life, you run the risk of arriving late to achieving your potential.

Is there something in life that you want to do, but you are too AFRAID to try it? Maybe you want to get a pilot's license, maybe you want to move into a new career, maybe you just want to begin living healthier. If you haven't tried it, how do you know that you will fail? What is keeping you from attempting something so important? And what or who, exactly, are you listening to? If you haven't tried, you haven't heard any sort of response; therefore, you must be listening to that nagging little voice inside you that tells you to be afraid. And that voice doesn't have the experience of trying yet. Remember, one of the obstacles of faith is fear, and fear must be conquered because destiny will always face resistance. Understand that and move past it.

Faith is, basically, confidence in God's word. It is carrying a belief that God is real and that this real God is intentional about His will dominating your life. In order to accept that, you have to live with a confidence that nothing exists that predates God, nothing exists that is stronger than God, and that God, for a reason mysterious to us, has chosen to rest His image in these frail vessels called human beings. He put treasure in us, and, as a result, our lives are simply to live in obedience to His gracious presence. It is also our job to attempt to inspire and compel others, by example in our own lives, to want faith in Him, which is what we should be enjoying. So nothing that life presents us ought to make us weaken the strong cords of our faith. We have to believe that God can and God will, and perhaps God already has done for us what needs to be done.

We have to believe that God can and God will, and perhaps God already has done for us what needs to be done.

Let Faith WAR against doubt.

When doubt is building permanent structures that obstruct your ability to function as you need to in life, faith reminds doubt that it has no permit to build on land owned by God, and it will be required to vacate the premises immediately. And, further, when doubt refuses to vacate, faith demonstrates the credentials to demand removal from the premises. In this way, faith is a warrior – a sentinel. After all, the Earth is the Lord's and only the Lord's, and there is only one God and He is a jealous God.

He will not allow anything else to occupy His Earth or His people and their faith. God is the author and finisher of faith. At His name, every knee shall bow; He is Alpha and Omega, the beginning and the end. Faith wars against everything opposite God's will for your life. That is a powerful and ever-present manifestation of proof that you should have no fear to proceed in anything you do, as long as you maintain that faith in God.

In the story of Moses as described in Exodus, faith warred against everything opposite the will of God. Amram and Jochebed were living in bondage in Egypt during a time when the Hebrews had so intimidated the Egyptians that Pharaoh wanted all Hebrew male newborns killed. When Jochebed gets pregnant and is fixated on the beauty of her newborn son, she hides him for three months despite Pharaoh's demands that all Hebrew male children be killed and, when she can't hide him anymore, she places him afloat along the Nile where, under God's providence, Moses is retrieved from the Nile by Pharaoh's daughter and reared in Pharaoh's house raised principally by his own mother. It is a story about which we are all familiar in the book of Exodus.

Moses grows in Pharaoh's house but with a pride for his own people; he is not suffering himself but is not at all removed from the suffering of his own kin. He truly empathizes with them. Therefore, he is always thinking about ways to progress and to defend them. Moses' privileged life never clouds his want of freedom for his own people or his feeling that he is being blessed to assist in their liberation. In fact, when he sees one of the Hebrews being beaten by an Egyptian, he steps in and things get so rough that he ends up killing the Egyptian and buries the body. As a result, he is forced to leave Egypt and years later, returns, having been called by God from a spiritual encounter on a remote hillside. While remarkable, what Moses goes onto achieve without fear is more remarkable. As a mature man, Moses has grown in his liberation approach; he no longer seeks to kill one Egyptian at a time but to spar spiritually with the Egyptian leader Pharaoh, a much greater feat. As a result, he and the Hebrews make their Exodus and sojourn in the wilderness for 40 plus years until, finally, Moses sees the land of promise and dies soon after, thereby passing the Hebrews entrance into Canaan onto Joshua. Talk about a life without fear. A life with faith.

Moses as a "Model of Faith"

Moses was a man who overcame fear. He used faith to war against everything not in God's will. The outcome of his fearless faith was great and has become a model for all Christians to live by.

To recap this remarkable story: By faith Moses was hidden for three months when he was born by his parents. They saw he was a beautiful child, and they were not afraid of the king's command. Here, they exhibited a courageous faith, a defiant faith – even a stubborn faith. By faith, Moses, when he became of age, refused to be called the son of Pharaoh's daughter. Again, what courageous faith – that defiant faith has come back – he is not afraid at all. By faith, Moses forsakes Egypt, not fearing the wrath of the king. By faith, he kept the Passover and the sprinkling of blood lest he who destroyed the firstborn should touch them. By faith, they passed through the Red Sea as if it was dry land, whereas the Egyptians attempting to do so were drowned. Remarkable and, yes, an example to us all. A model for how we should proceed in life. Faith like this results in progress in your own life, in your church, and in your community.

Faith is not safe!

We struggle with faith because faith is always putting security in question, and putting comfort in question, and putting convenience in question. It is hard to simply trust in God and proceed when your rational mind is sometimes telling you to do otherwise. Know this, however; you can't exercise faith and want to be safe, because God is always putting those with faith up against modern-day Pharaohs and in front of liberation movements and in the center of cultural progress. You don't walk by faith because you want safety; you walk by faith because you trust it is better being out in the sea of risk with God than on the shore of safety without Him. I trust God in a storm more than I trust myself without Him on the shore in the sunshine. I trust God in trouble more than I trust people in a calm environment. This is where we all need to be.

You don't walk by faith because you want safety; you walk by faith because you trust it is better being out in the sea of risk with God than on the shore of safety without Him.

Back when Hilary Clinton and Barack Obama were making their historic run for the White House, they had to proceed in areas that made them feel unsure and unsafe. As the first woman and the first African-American to make such successful attempts at the presidency, they were both navigating uncharted waters, so to speak. In so many early polls, Clinton was doing well in her ability to reach people on issues that were important such as the war, healthcare, important tax restructuring, racial inclusion, and depleted natural world resources, but Americans were still nervous when it came to values and honesty. On the other hand, Barack Obama, who was also doing well on early debates and issues, suddenly pulled ahead in a category that was critically important to the election. Instead of sticking to the common path and talking generally about issues that were debated over and over again by ALL politicians, he began to cut to the heart of the matter. He used his faith and he tackled some difficult and trying issues head-on. That, in the end, was what the public, the American people, needed. As a result, he was elected the Democratic candidate by his party and, eventually, President of the United States by a landslide.

Don't refuse faith.

We are all going to encounter modern-day "Pharaohs" in our lives. Would we all be able to hear that Pharaoh and hide Moses anyway? Would we be afraid of what keeping Moses alive might mean? Giving into that fear is, basically, a refusal of faith. So many people today have defeatist attitudes. They don't cut to the heart of the matter. They vacillate when it comes to doing the right thing. We can't accept life as depressing, or allow injustices on so many levels – racial, social and spiritual – to go unaddressed. Tackle these issues head-on, make a difference, change your life, and change the world. Faith must resist the temptation to conform to the low ambition of the world.

Don't resist faith.

Not only is there the refusal of faith, but there is also the resistance of faith. In Hebrews 11:24-26, we know that Moses, by faith, when he came of age, refused to be called the son of the Pharaoh's daughter, choosing rather to suffer affliction with the people of God as opposed to a life of ease and privileged reward. Moses could have had a life of privilege, no suffering, and no separation from power, at least Egyptian power. But his faith gave him principles and conviction and allowed him to prioritize what had to be done. Beyond that, faith made him realize what was right and what he had to do.

Our lesson here is a simple one: Only faith can help you see and accept that there is a reward that is greater than living in Pharaoh's house. In Hebrews 11:26, we hear that Moses was motivated by faith not to sit comfortable in Pharaoh's house. His faith allowed him to see the greater reward. His reward was born of obedience to God. We, too, can only live in obedience to God if we are walking by faith. Do not resist your reward. Do not reproach faith. Understand that, once you move forward, just like Moses left Pharaoh's house, you cannot go back. This life of faith without fear becomes a way of life.

This, ultimately, is our struggle as human beings, isn't it? We don't struggle with the desire to move forward or to get ahead; we struggle with making progress and then feeling like going back. We can't accept the change. We fear the unknown. Most of us will move forward asking God, "should I go back?", "Did I do the right thing?" It was the temptation of the Hebrews that God had to keep addressing and it is our temptation now. How can you know you are doing the right thing? Listen to your faith and proceed without fear, ALWAYS knowing there is no going back.

> *Listen to your faith and proceed without fear,*
>
> *ALWAYS knowing there is no going back.*

Moses saw a lot of suffering, but he saw a lot of good too. He watched God protect Hebrew children who had blood sprinkled on their doorpost while Egyptian male children were being destroyed. He watched God divide waters and the children of Israel walk through on dry ground, but he also watched God release the waters and Pharaoh's army drown in the red sea. In the end, he faced Pharaoh and the reward was deliverance:

- Faith brought him to a confrontation.
- Faith brought him out of Egypt.
- Faith brought him through the wilderness.
- Faith brought him to the border of Canaan.

Can you accept that Pharaoh is no longer a threat; that the wilderness is no longer your path? Can you change all you've known for so long for the better? Can you accept that this substandard life is over and you now have to find the life that faith in God has created? I think you can.

Chapter 14: *Faith to Fix the Heart*

Christians who are living blessed know that the more
they have, the greater the attacks on them can be.
I think many of us have either experienced this or
witnessed it. Have you ever had something fantastic
happen to you only to have others become jealous
of you and your blessings or your good fortune?
Have you ever lost a friend over a misunderstanding
involving money or prestige? Have you ever been the
target of gossip when you had things go your way
for once? You must be prepared to face and live with
recurring battles when you are blessed. You may
have to live with certain recurring battles because
you are blessed. Having such blessings is a good
thing, and with time and faith, learning to offset
attacks and naysayers is not as difficult. Embrace the
good in life and celebrate your blessings because they
do move you closer as opposed to further from God
as some would have you believe.

The Early Church

The early church experienced this dichotomy. While experiencing tremendous numerical and spiritual growth, they were also persecuted for their belief system. In the midst of this growth, they had seasons of fierce, repeated attacks. Most of this hostility was founded on the suspicion that Jesus, whom all these believers followed and for whom they endured tremendous suffering, was not a true Messiah. These naysayers believed the amazing stories about Him were gross exaggerations. In fact, these early followers of Jesus were persecuted because their growth was symbolic of a significant spiritual shift taking place in their time. Word was spreading quickly on the streets, and those who hated these believers in Christ could not create a spiritual design to combat the excitement being generated by this early church and their ministry and message.

However, the early followers of the church found it difficult to properly interpret what was happening within their own movement – the dissention and unrest that occurred when practices out of the norm were suggested. For example, when Paul becomes a primary figure in the movement, he says that he has been called by God to be an apostle to the Gentiles[1]. This was fine except that he began condoning a change in some very traditional practices such as ceremonial circumcision of young male babies, which did upset Jewish elders and scholars at the time. Many of these practices were what the Jews were accustomed to attaching to their faithfulness to the Lord, and they were now being held in tension regarding the Gentiles being close to Jesus without many of the same practices. Further, it was being implied that Paul believed and shared that the Gentiles would then be closer to God than the Jews given these new practices. This was, of course, scandalous. When those of the Jewish faith found out that Paul was not demanding that converted gentiles be circumcised, they called a council meeting to discuss rendering judgment regarding what corrective measures needed to take place.

Paul and Barnabas are in Jerusalem to defend their leadership of the fast-growing gentile ministry movement that didn't condone circumcision. Paul and Barnabas defend well and when they finish, the council goes into session, and Peter stands in support of Paul's work. This is a bold and difficult statement at the time because the Jews and the Gentiles are seeking and gaining favor from God in different ways. There is a struggle of sorts regarding who is in higher standing with the Lord. Whose practices are "right"?

Peter's Message to the Masses

Peter speaks to those who are in private session trying to make a decision after hearing Paul and Barnabas defend the integrity of their leadership in this new movement. He says, "Jesus made no distinction between us and them, for He purified their hearts by faith"[2].

Peter has heard the testimony of Paul and Barnabas and, therefore, suggests that the Gentiles are, indeed, an example of the work of God. Their lives are different, their hearts have been converted, their minds transformed, and they have been born into the kingdom. The Lord is working in their lives and he suggests that the Lord has purified them through their faith. He suggests that they are not unlike the Jews; their message warrants listening and trying to understand them.

This is interesting. He says that their lives were cleansed by the presence of Jesus Christ, but what brought them to this cleansing was their faith. We know now that God works on us and through us as we offer our faith to Him, and the wider, taller, and deeper our faith, the greater the impact of the Lord's presence in our lives. If we are experiencing the power of God at work in our lives, we should not doubt the Lord's ability to perform His will in our lives. We should always look, first, at the level of our faith and determine that God has the power to do anything and everything to make us who we are purposed to be in life. It seems, though, that the question always remains: Do I have the faith, the trust, the confidence in God – do I have the belief that he can do it all for ME?

In other words, it has to be your trust in God that puts you in a place where you can live like Jesus did when He trusted His Father and died for our sins, died with the promise of eternal life at Calvary. He went freely, with confidence in His Father, allowing faith and trust to guide Him towards an agenda and a path that did not synchronize with what He felt He wanted or needed in this life. He went and He saw where this faith was taking Him. Faith is the only discipline that puts you in position for God's will to be completely done in your life. You are only going to be who God wants you to be in faith, you are only going to accomplish what God wants you to accomplish in faith, and you will only defeat what is trying to defeat you in faith. You are, in other words, at your best when you are living with strong faith. Strong faith will produce a strong life.

We should always look, first, at the level of our faith and determine that God has the power to do anything and everything to make us who we are purposed to be in life.

Allowing God to give us a Clean Life through Faith

We all have habits that we know won't win us any spiritual rewards, but our routines keep us living with these bad habits – these bad practices that become second nature and difficult to abolish from our lives. Do we begrudge people what they have? Are we intolerant of others? Do we judge before we listen to another's story? We know we should let it go; we know we should walk away. We know we should fight these urges harder. We even know it's not good, nor productive, but it is a comfortable way to live, and, apparently, we don't have the faith to imagine life without these habits.

Beyond possessing these habits, we believe that we have cleansed them on our own. Most of us feel that we will never be a totally clean vessel for Christ if we are depending on ourselves to take on this monumental task. And that is true. We do need to accept God and trust in Him to be clean; however, there is a difference between being clean and changing habits. We do have the power to change bad habits. We have the power to become better people. Once we show the fortitude and the resolve needed to change our bad ways, we are open to the Holy Spirit and can begin to live a clean life with God.

Faith is the only discipline that puts you in position for God's will to be completely done in your life.

Living clean is the work of God in our lives as we surrender our exposed selves to Him. Peter says this is done though faith. So here is my point, if you want to sincerely clean your life up and truly offer God your newly changed life as a vessel fit for His glory, then you don't need to concentrate on the area you need to cleanse; you simply need to concentrate on intensifying your trust and confidence in God. God will hear you and He will cleanse what you don't have the power to. Remember that Peter said The Lord cleanses us from the inside out as we trust and believe Him.

In fact, the text says He purifies us, and isn't that what we want? To live pure for God?

I recently moved my family from a house we had been in for years. One of the most painful parts of the preparation was cleaning out belongings stored up from seven years in the same house. I had accumulated items I had forgotten I had. Some of it I had not seen in years! I found things that I had forgotten about, so I had gone out and bought the same item, duplicating purchases and wasting money. As I looked through these items – things I had lived without for years – things I didn't know I had, I still tried to convince myself that I needed them, that they had to move with us. I simply did not want to let these things go! I kept trying to tell myself that there was no harm in taking all this with me. It wouldn't make the boxes too heavy. No one would even know, but... did I need any of it? Why not make a clean break and start fresh? So I did; I dumped it all. To Peter's point, we have to attach faith to the process of our lives being cleaned up, because you need to trust and have confidence in God. You need to trust that what He is washing away from your life, you don't need to live effectively for Him.

Now all this is easy until you are wrestling with God about something He is washing away that you want Him to leave alone. Why would God wash this away? Why is He making me suffer? Trust that God knows that your interest or your involvement in something that you find tremendously valuable may create a hunger for something more damaging, may create access to a path that you shouldn't take. You can't know this, but God does. Your opinion of what it takes to clean your life is different than God's, I promise you. We base our decisions on what makes us happy and what makes us feel good. What appears to be innocent and what doesn't appear harmful or what keeps us focused and what helps us to help other people are noble, but this path may be different from what God uses to determine how we get "washed" or cleansed for a life of faith.

Keep in mind; You can't determine whether you are clean or worthy enough by looking at someone else's life and then determining that you don't do what they do – or, not as much as they do – or, on the other hand, that you are not as bad or as desperate as they are. We have discussed in past chapters and thus far in this chapter that God sees us as individuals; He cleanses us based upon how He intends to use us. He cleanses us for sacred use. He knows how He wants to use us, and then He washes you for that purpose. It's that simple. Just as you can't compare your life to another's (what he has, what she doesn't have, what you wish you had, etc.), you can't look at God's intent for others and compare it to your own destiny. That's why you can't get away with what others get away with because the nature of their sacred use is different from yours. You can't embrace what others embrace because the way God wants to use you is different.

Again, what opens you for this is faith. You have to trust God and have confidence in Him that He is working and washing and cleansing and purifying based upon the sacred usage He has for you. And since we don't always know the complete ways in which God will use us, we have to most times accept the cleansing process for what we don't yet know is purpose. I have to let God cleanse me before I understand why.

What conclusions can we draw from this?

What is encouraging about this? It doesn't seem like we've discussed anything that warrants getting excited about a life in faith – a life cleansed to be with God. It's like that little boy who runs into the house and has had so much fun playing in the dirt but … when it's time to get clean, feels like the fun has ended. He doesn't want to be washed – that's no fun. It requires effort, and it takes time. Besides, like that little boy, we like playing in the dirt, where there is more excitement than in the narrow confines of the bathtub. There is nothing exciting about this, right? Well… that's where we're all wrong.

We may not like the cleansing, but we can't help but to get excited that God is only cleansing us because God wants to use us. If He didn't have a use for us, He could let us stay dirty and die corrupted. God has a sacred purpose for all of us and chooses different ways to cleanse us. Purpose is why:

- David couldn't live as King without dealing with his affair with Bathsheba.

- Moses couldn't just sit on a hillside, watching sheep.

- Jeremiah couldn't just decide he wasn't going to preach.

- God touched Isaiah's tongue with a live coal.

- God dislocated Jacob's hip after he wrestled all night long.

- Jesus let Peter sink beneath those waves, and let the disciples fail at healing that father's sick son.

God refuses to let you live any way you want to when He has sacred purpose for you. He needs you:

- To show others how faith lives.

- To lead people to promise lands.

- To help people cross over into the land of purpose and power.

- To kill giants and stand up against wicked kings.

- To share dreams and to heal brokenness.

- To walk on water and feed multitudes.

- To preach the gospel and to make disciples and baptize believers.

- To teach the word of God.

- To be an instrument of praise.

Trust Him. Believe in Him. Have confidence that He is working on you to make you what He can use. Trust Him to give you a clean heart. Trust Him to make you what will honor Him.

You can't determine whether you are clean or worthy enough by looking at someone else's life and then determining that you don't do what they do – or not as much as they do – or, on the other hand – that you are not as bad or as desperate as they are.

Endnotes

1 *Acts 21:19*

2 *Acts 15:9*

Chapter 15: *When Faith takes it Out of Your Hands*

We all pray for God's help and guidance on occasion. However, are any of us guilty of having some preconceived notions of how that help should come or what type of guidance we'd like to get? Are we really willing to accept God's determination – His will – when times, for us, are trying? Or, do we want to hear or feel one thing and... turn our backs or refuse to listen if we hear another? It's important to consider that we should listen to God and trust in him in order to reach our full potential and fulfill our life's goals.

The Pharaoh's Dangerous Decree

Egypt had been a safe refuge for the Hebrews while Joseph and the Pharaoh, with whom he had an arrangement, were both still alive. Jacob and his sons found refuge in Egypt just before seven years of severe famine that would virtually wipe out any weak peripheral communities in the shadow of mighty Egypt[1]. Joseph, by this time, had positioned himself well despite all the attempts to suppress his gifts and leadership; he has become second in charge in the land to Pharaoh himself, and he negotiates for his kin to have Goshen, the best plot in Egypt. This arrangement is solid until Joseph dies and then his allied Pharaoh dies. A new Pharaoh rises in Egypt at a time when the Hebrews are as strong as they have ever been and they are steadily multiplying, and the Egyptians are not being silent about the fact that they are intimidated by the growing Hebrews and they want their new Pharaoh to handle this in a decisive way.

He attempts to do this; he instructs the midwives, who have been helping the Hebrew women when they are giving birth to their children, to observe the gender of the child. If it's a female, they are to let her live, and if it's a male they are to kill the male child. However, when Pharaoh issues this decree, he is unaware of the fact that the two midwives, while excellent at their jobs, are not good at what they do because they are loyal to him; they are, in fact, good at what they do because they love God. Instead of killing the male children, they let them live. When Pharaoh finds out, he asks them what they are doing and they cover it this way: They say to him, we can't keep up with these Hebrew women and the strength they have; they are dropping babies faster than we can get to them[2].

Pharaoh issues another decree that every male child should be set afloat along the Nile river to float to their demise. And in the season when this is taking place, two Levites, Brother Amran and Sister Jochebed, have been in love, serving God, and raising their two children Miriam and Aaron, when Jochebed discovers that she is again pregnant. She gives birth to young Moses, and when she looks at him, she sees the beauty that God has given him and, in their day, beauty was a sign of divine favor. She concludes that God must have a special purpose for this boy to let him be born with such presence. She and Amran talk, and they decide that it's worth the risk of their own lives, and their family's existence to try to save their little boy. For three months, they are successful; they do what's necessary to ensure that his cries are not heard. She feeds him from her breast without anyone noticing that she is nursing a newborn. They monitor who enters their home. They don't go out among the community too often during these three months, and they teach Miriam and Aaron how to move through the community without giving away the family secret. For three months, no one notices.

It gets extremely difficult, however, due to house searches and other intrusions. Also, there are probably rumors in the community of a baby crying late at night. Also, parents have certain intuitions, and they may have known, with every passing day, that they run the risk of this boy being discovered and killed. Of course, they are too attached to lose him now; they love their little boy. If they couldn't give him up at birth, they sure can't give him up after three months.

The Bible says, however, that Jochebed takes young Moses down to the Nile river and she makes a float of straw and tar[2], and places infant Moses in the river and turns to walk away. Her daughter, Miriam, however, stays within eye shot of her little brother floating and she notices that Pharaoh's daughter goes down to the river to bathe and discovers Moses. The Pharaoh's daughter has immediate compassion for this baby, and, in fact, says, "this is one of the Hebrew children" yet keeps him safe. Miriam sees this as an opportunity, and she jumps out and asks Pharaoh's daughter, "Do you want me to get a Hebrew woman to come and take care of this child for you?"[3] Pharaoh's daughter says yes, and Miriam goes home and alerts her mother, telling her that the Pharaoh's daughter has found a baby and is need of help to raise him. Jochebed gets up from the bed where she had been laying in the pool of her own tears, and she runs down and takes her son out of Pharaoh's daughter's hand and raises him. A miracle? Or did Jochebed simply obey God and reap this wonderful reward? Moses, certainly, was safe in her hands in the first place, but was not as safe until she released him and then got him back. She had to have tremendous faith to let her child go, trusting and hoping that he would live.

Why didn't God just allow hiding Moses to be sufficient safety? They had not been discovered; they had not been given up. Why make Jochebed go through the emotional trauma of thinking that she may never see or hold her child again? Did God have big plans for Moses? We know now He did. Did He need to communicate to Jochebed that Moses would be safer in God's hands? That did turn out to be true. Once released, he lived happy and safe, a privileged child of the Pharaoh and his loving birth mother by his side.

How often do we wrestle with "the right thing to do?"

How much, do you surmise, has been lost or altered – even destroyed – because you would not let God take it out of your hands? Decisions, relationships, priorities, problems? How many times was your faith not mature enough to trust God to work without your hands being on a project, a plan, something important to you?

Faith can take you to a place where you trust God to work even if He takes partnership of its resolution out of your hands. In other words, you ought to trust God enough to release what is precious to you, even though you want it more than life itself, and believe that God will manage what you release to Him in such a way that He will give it back **or** make you powerful and purposeful without it. I'm sure there are times when you want God to shout

out the instructions and tell you what to do to fix something in your life to fortify it, to make it right. Remember to look closely – to see God with hands extended, telling you to trust Him – to give it up and allow Him to give it back – or to decide your fate for the better. Jochebed is an example of this. She releases Moses in the Nile and doesn't know for sure if she will ever see him again. And yet she does so with faith, believing that God is real and that He is a rewarder of those who diligently seek Him.

Some of what you have, you can't keep until you give it up to God. Some of what you carry in terms of dreams and ambitions and goals, you can't have to work to reality until you are willing to give them up to God's will and creative design. Some of what you desire will never find you until you are willing to give that desire up and then God will fill it or replace it.

How do we accomplish this? Jochebed releases Moses to the Nile River, because she knew that releasing him was a part of trusting God. She felt that she was not taking her hands off of such a dire situation because she was giving up; she was taking her hands off of it because she was giving in to God's will. This is the next level of faith. It's the ability to trust God to do what God does without our input; to love Him enough to totally surrender something important, knowing we are important enough to Him that He will make our priorities His priority.

How many of us now think that "release" means that we are giving up? How many of us don't see how it's going to work out? I'm telling you: Release it to God, and it will all be clear. This is a challenge. Jochebed put so much into building that basket, knowing that she might be doing that for Moses and he will still die. How do we, then, put that effort into something, hand it to God and wonder that it might not work out? Well, as we discussed, when you turn it over to God, you want to turn over the best of your effort and the best of your belief, and the best of your energies. God understands that; you have given Him something that was in condition enough to be blessed. Trust that He will know what to do. Trust that what happens will be for the best.

What is your basket? What do you need to stay afloat? You can't rely on drugs, alcohol or destructive behavior that can damage you and your family. You have to spend some energy on making sure your basket can stay afloat. This way, God will see that care I talked about earlier – He will see what a priority these things are in your life, and He will act accordingly. God wants your best presentation – the best "you".

Take the issue of marriage both in our churches and in this culture today, in general. It almost appears that marriage is under attack these days – young people ready to divorce over small issues – further decrees issued by modern day "Pharaohs" who glamorize non-monogamous marriages through television and other mediums. As a society, we have tried to protect the institution of marriage only to lose again and again. We need to place our marriages in the modern day basket, releasing them to God and His will. We also need to be mindful of what kind of "basket" we use to reach God. Is it a basket of resentment, anger, bitterness and the need for revenge? Is it full of character assassination or worse, hatred? God wants to bring reconciliation, but if you want to present him with a "basket" full of venom, He will assign priority accordingly. Instead, we need to stay prayerful, open, sensitive and intimate with God. In this way, He will answer our call to save marriage in this day and age.

Further, Amran and Jochebed discovered that when you release what you have to the Lord, He works on it and returns it to you without the worry previously attached to it. For example, before she released Moses, Jochebed had to worry about how to protect him; however, after she released Moses, she didn't have to be afraid to present him. She could walk with him in public and didn't have to fear for his life. Maybe that's why Jesus says, "if you want to save your life then lose it to Me, and if you want to be the first then be the last"[4]. The greatest thing we can do to bring purpose to our lives is to turn our lives and everything in them over to Him.

I am intrigued by those shows in which somebody is involved in a tragic accident, and he or she are rushed into emergency and then into intense surgery. The plot thickens as we wait; we even get to sit with the family while they wait those long, excruciating periods of time for the doctor to come out and then….. after hours of waiting and huddling among loved ones, the doctor emerges from the OR, wipes his brow and pulls down his mask and says, "Well, we have done everything we can do. We have your loved one stable, but it's out of our hands now." And the family looks worried like they have just entered the worst part of the scenario. I stand up in whatever room I am in and try to shout through the television screen, "Don't get worried when the doctor says that! What he means is that after they have done all they can and didn't mess it up, they are leaving the rest to God. Now you can be confident that God's will can do what it needs to do. Now it's time to start calling people, telling them the doctors didn't blow it; they gave God something to work with, and we are expecting miracles any moment now." We should be encouraged in such scenarios – not fearful.

We know now that God grants you access to faith. God tests your faith. God expects you to hand over your faith to Him. And God will perform miracles with this life of yours.

Live this way from now on. Trust that:

- God understands you.

- God loves you.

- God knows better than you do what is good for your life.

- God expects you to question now and then, but He also expects you to be prayerful and introspective.

- God wants you to look to the Bible for your examples and learn from those who have gone before you.

- God knows you can be the best you can be everyday in this life.

Endnotes

1 *Exodus 1:1-11*

2 *Exodus 2:3,4*

3 *Exodus 2:7*

4 *Luke 9:24; Mathew 20:16*

In Summary

Faith is often an elusive concept to fit into our busy, modern lives. We do believe in God, and we do give a portion of our lives to Him in many ways: Every Sunday in church; when we pray before we go to bed at night; and even when we reflect on both our blessings and our challenges on a daily basis. In fact, there are many places in our lives in which we allow faith to remain prevalent; however, it seems that when life gives us change, strife, success – basically, movement in any way, we retreat into our respective routines, and we refuse to embrace God's message to us out of complacency, stubbornness or fear.

We know now that God does provide us access to His grace and love, and it is purely up to us whether or not we participate in His offerings. Through Him, we can know true faith, and we can enjoy the blessings of His love as "rewarder" of our devotion. We know, too, that it is ok to speak to God – to ask Him for help in substantiating or even fortifying our faith when we find that we can't be as gracious as we need to be or when we discover that we are being persecuted for the life that we lead. This is an easy concept to grasp and, once we let go of any fear that we might have, it is a clear pathway to follow.

Applying this newfound, unfaltering faith to our daily lives can require ongoing maintenance and reflection, however. It's not easy to hand our hopes, dreams and ambitions to God. It is even more difficult to let go of our fear and venture outside of our respective safety zones. When we do, however, we can enjoy a life lived to its fullest. We can reach the potential for which God feels we are destined.

Living with faith, and living that faith without fear, is quite a concept to grasp; after all, we might think we have faith, and we might even think that we know how we want God to call us or what we want Him to say to us when we ask the hard question, "why me, God?" However, we can't know what God has planned for us, and we can't reap the rewards of a life lived in faith until we completely trust in God's wisdom. We have to seek He who grants us our destiny. We have to do that without fear. And, certainly, by now, we all know we are capable and worthy.

About William H. Curtis

Reverend Dr. William H. Curtis is the Senior Pastor of Mt. Ararat Baptist Church, located in the East Liberty neighborhood of Pittsburgh, Pennsylvania. The church and Dr. Curtis are revered and trusted members of the urban community there, developing and serving the neighborhood.

A native of Baltimore, Maryland, Reverend Curtis accepted a call to ministry at the age of 17. He has a Bachelor of Arts Degree in Religious Studies and Philosophy from Morgan State University, a Master of Divinity Degree from The Howard University School of Divinity, and a Doctor of Ministry Degree from the United Theological Seminary in Dayton, OH. Dr. Curtis' commitment to excellence through education is a direct result of his experience and innate understanding regarding how to communicate the teachings of history and theology to others, not only as a lifelong student and multi-degreed preacher of the gospel, but also as an effective, down to earth teacher in practical real life application of the gospel.

Reverend Curtis has been at Mt. Ararat Baptist Church in Pittsburgh, Pennsylvania since 1997. Under his direction, the church has grown from 400 members to over 8,500 with four worship services each weekend. His ministry has led to several landmark events at Ararat, including the formation of a Community Development Corporation to minister to the greater Pittsburgh area and the liquidation of the church mortgage in a one-day "Harvest Sunday" offering. He also implemented a Community Tithe Program, which returns over 10% of the congregation's offering to the surrounding community.

Dr. Curtis is as one of the most well-known, preachers in the United States. His spiritual wisdom, academic background and continued community influence has earned him many honors, among them participation in a national "think-tank" forum with former President Clinton, inclusion in a book entitled, "Outstanding Black Sermons, Volume Four" edited by Dr. Walter S. Thomas, and the opportunity to minister to a number of political and community forums throughout the City of Pittsburgh. Dr. Curtis currently serves on the Board of the Urban League of Pittsburgh, is a member of the African American Leadership Committee and has served as President of Hampton University Ministers' Conference for a number of years.

In 2001, Dr. Curtis founded William H. Curtis Ministries, a grassroots organization with plans to expand his ministry throughout the United States and overseas. Dr. Curtis is an expert in using faith to counsel and improve the lives of people in all areas of their lives.

Dr. Curtis is married to the former Christine Y. Richardson, and they are the proud parents of one daughter, Houston.